KOKOLOGY

The Game of Self-Discovery

Tadahiko Nagao and Isamu Saito

A Fireside Book
Published by Simon & Schuster
New York London Toronto Sydney Singapore

FIRESIDE
Rockefeller Center
1230 Avenue of the Americas
New York, NY 10020

Originally published in Japan by Seishun Publishing Co., Ltd.,
1–12 Wakamatsu-cho, Shinjuku-ku, Tokyo, as
SOREIKE KOKOLOGY © 1998

FIRESIDE and colophon are registered trademarks
of Simon & Schuster, Inc.

Designed by Liane Fuji

Manufactured in the United States of America

10

Library of Congress Cataloging-in-Publication Data
Nagao, Tadahiko.
[Sore ike kokoroji. English]
Kokology : the Japanese path to self-knowledge / Tadahiko
Nagao and Isamu Saito.
p.   cm.
Originally published as: Soreike kokology. Tokyo :
Seishun Pub. Co., © 1998.
1. Psychology. I. Title: Soreike kokology. II. Saito, Isamu, date.
III. Title.
BF149 . N2513 2000
158—dc21   00-036575

ISBN 0-684-87148-3 (Pbk.)

THE KOKOLOGY PROJECT TEAM

WRITERS	Tadahiko Nagao and Isamu Saito
EXECUTIVE PRODUCER	Hisataka Saito
GENERAL PRODUCER	Tadahiko Nagao Takanori Ikeda
TEAM STAFF	Shinichi Iwata Daisuke Shidara
COOPERATOR	Keiko Higashiomori
ILLUSTRATOR	Makoto Ishizuki
TRANSLATOR	Douglas Sipp, Office Miyazaki, Inc.
SPECIAL THANKS TO	James C. Vines Seiichiro Shimono Hisako Ishizuki Toshihide Ochiai Takeshi Itoh
SUPERVISOR	Isamu Saito

CONTENTS

CONTENTS

KOKOLOGY 101

kokology \ kō kōl´ ō jē \ *n* [Japanese, *kokoro*, mind, spirit, feelings + Greek, *-logia*, the study of] **1.** A series of psychological games designed to uncover emotional and behavioral traits of the players **2.** A popular term for the interpretation of the hidden meanings of human behavior and situational responses — **kokologist** *n* — **kokological** *adj* — **kokologize** *vi*

A WORD FROM PROFESSOR SAITO

T he eyes of the mind peer in two directions. One faces the outside world, gathering information about the environment and the people around us. The other is turned inward and looks at the hidden world of the inner self. This is the eye you use to survey the workings of your own mind, to ponder what others might be thinking, and to gaze into the future and foresee the kind of person you may one day become.

Many forms of media, such as books, newspapers, and television, have been developed to help people learn about and understand the outside world. It could be said that the media explosion of recent years has created a state of sensory and information overload, where every day we are faced with more data than we can possibly assimilate. But there are far fewer media to help us explore and understand the world within. Psychological games are one such medium, designed to help open the inner eye and sharpen its sight. The science of psychology itself allows people to study and comprehend the mind, but like any science, it demands time, hard work, and dedication to learn and uses a specialized vocabulary that keeps many nonspecialists at a distance. Kokology is a game based on the science of psychology, but with a fun and easy approach that makes it possible for everyone to experience and enjoy the world of the mind.

Kokology also works as a communications tool. For many people, the words *psychological test* evoke a dark or frightening image.

I'm a psychologist myself, and even *I* don't like to take them. But psychological games make the same process of discovery interesting and fun, and people feel less threatened when they view the experience as just a form of play. In Kokology it's okay to disagree with the interpretation of a quiz answer if it sounds crazy or unbelievable—that's part of the fun. But I think you'll find more often than not that you're surprised at how accurately the answers reflect people's true personalities, including your own. This makes the game a great way to bridge communication gaps between friends and lovers, to bring you closer together and help you understand each other better, to open up conversations on what might otherwise be difficult, sensitive, or forbidden subjects.

I have tried to make Kokology as entertaining as possible, while keeping true to the principles of psychological science. I hope you enjoy the time you spend playing and that you feel you've learned something about yourself and others in your life when you're done.

ISAMU SAITO
Professor, Rissho University

PLAYING THE GAME

When we set out to develop Kokology, our first and foremost goal was to make it fun. After all, who in their right mind would want to play a game that isn't? The basic concept was already there—our plan was to create a game where people would imagine themselves in everyday situations and unusual scenarios and respond to simple questions. The answers are interpreted from a psychological perspective and tell us something about the way that person's mind works. It's kind of like a Rorschach test that uses words instead of inkblots.

The concept was the easy part. The hard part was keeping the balance between science and fun. Professor Saito can vouch for the science; only you can be the judge of whether we've succeeded on the fun side. I'm not a psychologist myself, but I do understand enough about human nature to know that people don't like long introductions—especially not to a book of games. So I'm going to end by leaving you with a list of eight tips for making your experience with Kokology satisfying, enlightening, and fun.

Enjoy!

—TADAHIKO NAGAO

EIGHT TIPS FOR PLAYING KOKOLOGY

1. Say the first thing that pops into your head.
The games work best when you don't hesitate or agonize over your choice of words. There are no right or wrong answers, so just relax and say whatever springs to mind.

2. Play with other people if you can.
Kokology can be read alone like any other book, but it's most enjoyable, exciting, and entertaining when you play with a partner or in a group. It's a chance to have a few laughs and get to know each other better. You may find that you have more in common than you ever suspected. On the other hand, you may find you're so incompatible that it's as though you're from different planets. There's only one way to find out for sure.

3. Don't try to predict the answers.
It's natural to want to try to outsmart the quizzes or guess what their hidden meanings may be. But what are you going to learn from that?

4. Be honest with yourself.
Kokology may be only a game, but like any good game, it can teach you something about yourself if you let it. Don't be afraid to accept the truth when a minor fault or shortcoming of yours is exposed. I can sense that you're basically a good, intelligent, and likable person. You bought this book, didn't you?

5. Be prepared.

Some of the quizzes will ask you to write something down or draw a picture, so it's a good idea to have a pen or pencil and some paper handy before you start. Advanced-level Kokologists might want to try videotaping a round of games at the next office party. The expressions on people's faces when their true characters are revealed can be priceless. And the secrets they unwittingly blurt out might be worth good money, too.

6. Don't read ahead.

This goes along with the advice of not trying to guess the answers, but it's directed at the group that likes to read the last page of a mystery novel first. Why not open yourself up to a few surprises? Is it really so satisfying to be able to say, "Oh, I knew it all along"?

7. Watch people's reactions (including your own).

The interpretations to the scenarios given in this book are only a starting point for learning more about yourself and others. Sometimes it's more instructive (and entertaining) to see how someone reacts to an answer that's a bit off target than it is to read an interpretation that's right on the money.

8. Keep an open mind.

In Kokology, as in life, it's important to keep things in perspective. There are no correct answers and more than one way of reading any situation. If you're playing with friends, take the opportunity to learn from and about them. What fun would the world be if we all thought alike? Variety is the spice of life.

KOKOLOGY

A DESERT JOURNEY

Y our desktop is spilling over with unfinished paperwork;
the rest of the office has already gone home for the night.
You look up at the clock and it laughs back. You wonder, with a
sinking feeling inside, if this job will ever be done.

The professor drones on and on through a three-hour double
lecture on the world's most boring subject. There's no space left for
doodles in your notebook, and you're only thirty minutes into the
class. You begin to think you've somehow been frozen in time.

Waiting can be a special form of torture, worse than any momentary pain. The combination of frustration and boredom can
send even the bravest heart into a state of panic. Our first journey
will bring us face-to-face with the infinite. Take a moment to prepare yourself, and enter the eternal desert. . . .

1. You are riding a camel across the vast and empty expanse of a
seemingly endless desert. You have ridden until you are near ex-
haustion. What words would you say to the camel that has carried
you all the way?

2. Just at the point when you thought you'd die of thirst, a beautiful oasis appears. But someone has arrived before you. Who is this
other traveler? (Use the name of a person you know.)

3. Time passes slowly in the desert, and it feels like an eternity before the lights of a town appear on the horizon. You have finally reached your destination. What are your feelings as you come to your journey's end?

4. The time has come to part with the camel you have ridden for so long. Just as you dismount, a new rider climbs into the saddle to take your place. Who is the new rider? (Name another person in your life.)

KEY TO A DESERT JOURNEY

(T)he desert and camel theme symbolizes the journey toward personal independence. Specifically, this scenario reveals your feelings about parting with a lover. Your answers show how you might react when the time comes to go your separate ways.

1. The words you spoke to the camel reveal what you might say to yourself when you realize love has been lost. Did you try words of encouragement like "We'll make it through somehow!" or "Don't worry, this can't go on forever"? Or was there a hint of despair—"We're lost . . . this is hopeless . . . I think we're going to die out here"?

2. In psychological terms, the oasis symbolizes the key to solving one's problems. The person you encountered here could be someone who has helped or comforted you in the past or one you might turn to in times of need.

3. The town at journey's end stands for the order restored to your emotions once you've recovered from your broken heart. Your feelings upon reaching the town are your true feelings about finally getting over a lost love.

4. The new rider is a person toward whom you feel a secret rivalry, jealousy, or resentment. Is the person you named a rival in love or maybe someone who once broke your heart?

THE BLUE BIRD

O ne day a blue bird suddenly flies through a window into your room and is trapped. Something about this lost bird attracts you, and you decide to keep it. But to your surprise, the next day the bird has changed color from blue to yellow! This very special bird changes color again overnight—on the morning of the third day it is bright red, and on the fourth it turns completely black. What color is the bird when you wake up on the fifth day?

1. The bird doesn't change color; it stays black.
2. The bird turns back to its original blue.
3. The bird turns white.
4. The bird turns golden colored.

KEY TO THE BLUE BIRD

$\left(T\right)$he bird that flew into your room seemed like a symbol of good fortune, but suddenly it changed color, making you worry that happiness would not last. Your reaction to this situation shows how you respond to difficulties and uncertainty in real life.

1. Those who said the bird stays black have a pessimistic outlook.

Do you tend to believe that once a situation goes bad, it never really returns to normal? Maybe you need to try thinking, If this is as bad as it gets, it can't get any worse. Remember, there's no rain that doesn't end and no night so dark that there's no dawn the next day.

2. Those who said the bird turns blue again are practical optimists.

You believe that life is a mix of good and bad and that it doesn't pay to fight against that reality. You accept adversity calmly and let things run their course without undue stress or worry. This outlook lets you ride out the waves of adversity without being swept away.

3. Those who said the bird turns white are cool and decisive under pressure.

You don't waste time on fretting and indecision, even when a crisis develops. If a situation gets too bad, you feel it's better to cut your losses and look for another route to your goal rather than getting bogged down in needless grief. This proactive approach means that things seem to just naturally go your way.

4. Those who said the bird turns golden can be described as fearless.

You don't know the meaning of pressure. To you, every crisis is an opportunity. You might be compared with Napoleon, who said, ". . . impossible: the word is not French." But be careful not to let your boundless confidence get the best of you. It's a very fine line between fearless and foolhardy.

A NIGHT AT THE SYMPHONY

T here's something magical about a night at the symphony—
a sense of expectation and pure pleasure. Imagine being
able to take a place on that stage among the other musicians, a
once-in-a-lifetime chance to perform at your very best.

If you could join the orchestra, what instrument do you see
yourself playing?

1. Violin
2. String bass
3. Trumpet
4. Flute

KEY TO A NIGHT AT THE SYMPHONY

M usical instruments are symbolic of members of the opposite sex. The pairing of you and your instrument shows how you perceive yourself in making the music of love. The instrument you chose gives insight into what you think of as your strongest lovemaking technique.

1. Violin

The violin demands sensitive fingerwork and a delicate touch with the bow to draw forth music from the taut strings. You see yourself as having the same awareness and skill in locating and playing upon your partners' most sensitive points. There's a sense of adventure in the way your hands can create such beautiful music by running over the same familiar notes.

2. String bass

There's a feeling of power gotten from taking position behind an enormous bass and making it call out in a tremendous moan. In love, your skill rests in the ability to bend your partners to your will, taking complete control, and driving them onward to pleasures they never imagined they could experience. You never ask permission, but that dominating character is what makes you so irresistible.

3. Trumpet

There's no getting around it—your mouth is the strongest weapon in your arsenal. Whether it's whispering love talk in your partner's ear or exploring them with your lips, you have all the characteristics of the oral personality.

4. Flute

The flute demands incredible patience from those who want to master it. You show that same patience in the way you wear down partners with your persistence, determination, and stamina. Your lovers are often taken off guard when what they thought would be a brief recital quickly develops into a full concerto in six movements.

ON YOUR BIRTHDAY . . .

Y our birthday is the one day a year when you're justified in expecting things to be just a little nicer than usual. Well wishes and congratulations, presents and cards, maybe even a party or a romantic dinner for two.

It's your birthday today, and when you check your mailbox you see you've gotten a card from someone you would have never suspected. Who is the sender? You have also received a number of gifts from family and friends. Of that group, who sent you the biggest package? (Give the names of people in your life when answering this quiz.)

KEY TO ON YOUR BIRTHDAY . . .

$\left(T\right)$ he responses you gave signify your true feelings about people in your life, feelings you might not even be aware of yourself.

The person who unexpectedly sent you a card is actually someone you would like to care more about you or give you more attention. In short, the person you named as the sender is someone you worship from afar. Is it someone you barely know, someone you've been hesitant to approach, or just a friend you haven't heard from in a while? Maybe it's time you made the first move toward bridging that gap.

On the surface, you might associate the biggest package you received with good feelings about the sender. But from a psychological perspective, the person you named as the sender is actually someone whose affections you take for granted. This doesn't necessarily signify a lack of respect, but you definitely feel confident of their feelings for you. Be careful not to get overconfident. What feels like security to you may look like plain selfishness to others.

PICTURES AT AN EXHIBITION

very once in a while it's nice to take a break from your busy schedule and experience the world of art firsthand. Some of us go to concerts or plays, some take up dance or a musical instrument, others try their hand at crafts. And of course there's always a trip to a museum. . . .

You are standing in front of a painting at an art museum, hands clasped behind your back as you try to take it in, when a total stranger comes up alongside you and says something to you. Which of the following does the stranger say?

1. "Isn't that a beautiful picture?"
2. "What do you think of this painting?"
3. "Excuse me, do you have the time?"
4. "You know, I happen to be a painter myself."

KEY TO PICTURES AT AN EXHIBITION

(W)hen a stranger suddenly speaks to you there's always a momentary mix of apprehension and expectancy. In this imaginary scenario, the words the stranger spoke actually reflect how you react in chance encounters and when meeting others. Your answer reveals what kind of impression you make when meeting someone for the first time.

1. "Isn't that a beautiful picture?"

Your friendly and positive nature creates a great first impression on almost everyone you meet. Your only concern should be that people may not take you seriously at first.

2. "What do you think of this painting?"

You're the type who likes to feel out the other person's temperament before committing yourself to anything. People can sense that hesitancy, and it may color their reactions to you. You won't step on any toes with your cautious approach, but you may end up living on other people's terms.

3. "Excuse me, do you have the time?"

To half the world you seem like an all right sort, but to the other half you look just a little strange. You create a first impression of living life at your own pace and maintaining an individuality that some would call eccentric. You don't place much importance on what others may be thinking or feeling. For better or worse, therein lies the secret to you.

4. "You know, I happen to be a painter myself."

On first meeting someone, you come across as a little bit nervous and overeager. Maybe you're just trying too hard to be liked, but the harder you try, the worse an impression you make. Don't worry so much about making people think you're great—they'll like you better if you just loosen up and relax.

DEEP IN THE MOUNTAINS

The mountains and the sea—nature has a power that draws us to her. After all, we are all nature's children, born into her world and fed on her bounty. No matter what marvels technology may develop, getting back to nature lets us feel truly alive. Medical science may make advances, but the best medicine will always be nature's own healing power.

Your next journey will take you back to that green world, and what better setting for you to rediscover your natural self?

1. You have set off to climb a mountain, in search of a fabulously rare stone. What is your impression of the mountain as you stand at its foot?

2. After a hard search, you still haven't found the stone, and now the sun has fallen. What will you do next?

3. You have finally discovered the stone you were seeking. What kind of stone is it? Describe its size, weight, and value.

4. Now it is time to come down from the mountain and return home. What parting words do you have for the mountain, and what is its reply?

Tadahiko Nagao and Isamu Saito

KEY TO DEEP IN THE MOUNTAINS

(T) he mountain that looms before you represents your father, or a father figure in your life. In psychological terms, it is a manifestation of the archetype of the "wise old man." The stone you seek symbolizes abilities and strengths you must discover within yourself on your own journey to adult independence.

1. Your impression of the mountain shows the image you have of your father. Was it difficult and unforgiving? Gentle and easily conquered? Or did you have an idealized image of a magnificent peak that somehow seemed to welcome you and encourage you in your quest?

2. The stone you are searching for represents your as yet undiscovered talent or strength. Your response to this question shows whether you will ever realize that untapped potential.

People who say they'd keep searching for the stone no matter what tend to show the same persistence and determination in their own lives, never giving up even when efforts seem fruitless.

Those who said they'd call it quits for the day but come back again to continue the search are the type who pace themselves, spreading their efforts over a long period of time. There are probably more than a few late bloomers in this group.

People who gave up looking for the stone altogether are in danger of never fulfilling their true potential.

3. The way you described the stone shows your feeling of self-worth. How big and heavy was it, and what did you think of its value?

"Oh, about twenty dollars or so," Hmmm, that's not much of an appraisal, is it?

"It turned out to be a huge diamond worth millions!" Hold on now, let's not get carried away with ourselves.

4. Your parting words to the mountain reveal what you have always wanted, but never been able, to say to your father. The mountain's reply shows your idea about his feelings for you. Do you recognize any of these patterns?

You: "Thanks for everything."

Mountain: "You take care of yourself."

Did you have that kind of ideal exchange? Or did it go more like this:

You: "Well, it looks like I'm finally through with you."

Mountain: "You can say that again!"

Maybe it's time you and your father sat down for a talk.

The Forgotten Wallet

I t's a morning like any other: last-minute preparations before you run out the door. Hair? Check. Clothes? Check. Everything's ready to go. . . .

You get on your way at the usual time, but halfway to work you realize your wallet is not where you always keep it. A quick search confirms the worst—you left it at home! And there's no time for you to turn around and go back for it. You begin going through your pockets and bags to see how much spare cash you have to get you through the day. How much money do you find?

KEY TO THE FORGOTTEN WALLET

T he amount of cash you found represents the amount of money you forget about in your daily life; money you don't rely on being there. It also represents the amount of money you feel comfortable lending to others. Just how much did you say you found?

About ten or twenty dollars? That seems like a reasonable figure.

More than a hundred? You're probably popular with friends just before payday.

Nothing at all? Maybe you're broke, or are you just cheap?

Blue Coat, Yellow Coat

G athering in the town square for the lighting of the Christmas tree gives people a chance to come together as a community and celebrate the end of another year. It's a time of nostalgia and a chance for new memories to be born. People are in the holiday spirit, strangers act like friends, and a sense of peace is all around.

The night is cold, and you have come with a group of friends and acquaintances to watch the lighting of the tree. In the group of people with you, one person is wearing a yellow coat and another person is in blue. Who are the people wearing the blue and yellow coats? (Give the names of people you know.)

KEY TO BLUE COAT, YELLOW COAT

I n psychology, bright colors such as yellow are associated with warm and positive feelings, while cool colors like blue are linked with cold, negative emotions. It may surprise even you, but the person you named as wearing the yellow coat is someone you like or who makes you feel happy, while something about the person in the blue coat leaves you cold.

WRITTEN IN THE STARS

W hen you look up into a star-filled sky at night, sometimes it's possible to lose yourself in the infinite depths of space. We may be aware of their vast distances from earth, yet the stars still look like friendly messengers and granters of dreams when we see them twinkling in the dark. As the hours grow late, it's a comfort to look up and have their distant power to draw upon.

For this next game, you'll need paper and a pencil.

1. First, draw three stars of different sizes.
2. Next, draw a comet's tail on one (and only one) of your stars.

KEY TO WRITTEN IN THE STARS

(T) he stars combine a glittering image of the power to grant wishes and make dreams come true with a sense of distance and unattainability. Stars determine our present and give a hint of things to come. Your drawing illuminates your work life in general and your current career path in particular.

1. The largest star you drew represents the job you hold now, its potential and its disappointments. If the difference in size between that star and the other two is not very great, it signifies dissatisfaction or at least disinterest in your career, a willingness to shop around and keep your options open. Watch for an unexpected call from a headhunter. They have ways of finding these things out.

On the other hand, if your job star is much larger than the others, it indicates you're deeply absorbed and committed to your current path. Your concern should be not to fall into the trap of workaholism. All work and no play is no way to live.

2. In cultures throughout history and around the world, comets have been seen as harbingers of disaster and cataclysmic change. The star you gave a comet's tail to represents trouble looming on the horizon. If it's on one of the smaller stars, you're in luck; the heavens have overlooked you for now. But if your largest star is a comet, it might be a good time for you to bring your résumé up-to-date. The stars never lie.

Sweet Memories

What is it about reminiscences of childhood that stir the heart so deeply and make us long to turn back the clock? Is it that sense of returning to innocence or just the pleasure of feeling young again? Those were the days when every toy, doll, and game was a special kind of treasure. The collector's mania for antiques and memorabilia has its roots in these childhood fascinations and the desire to relive the past, if only for a short while.

Our next encounter will take us back to that simpler time, to a little candy shop down the street. Perhaps you'll find your younger self among the goods in stock.

1. Inside the candy store, you find rows and rows of the old familiar candies, chocolate bars, chewing gums, and sweets from your youth. Some are stacked in organized shelves, some are loose in baskets and jars. What candy do you pick first, and why did you choose it? (Give the full reason behind your choice.)

2. While you're wandering the store making selections, you notice that outside a group of children look as though they're getting ready to enter the store. How many children actually come in?

3. You make your purchases and go home with a bag of candy. But when you open the bag, you see that the shopkeeper has added

some free extra candies as a special treat for you. How many extras did you get?

4. You've been thinking about giving the candy you bought as a gift to someone. To whom, if anyone, would you give it?

KEY TO SWEET MEMORIES

(T) he candy theme harkens back to the time in your life when you could count on an occasional treat and even expect to be spoiled. This scenario reveals your expectations of others and your level of dependence.

1. What did you choose first from the almost endless selection? More important, why did you choose it? The reasoning behind your choice actually shows what you desire most from other people.

If you thought something like "I'd take the one with the secret toy surprise in the pack" you're likely the type who responds well to people bearing gifts. (And, turning that around, you might not be so positive toward those who turn up empty-handed.) Beware of becoming too materialistic. There's more to life than trading cards, iron-ons, and secret decoder rings.

If you said you chose the candy because you remember how good it tasted or it made you feel nostalgic, you are hungry for the same attention and affection you received from your mother as a child. Men, if you answered this way, you may be looked on as something of a mama's boy.

If you made your decision based on external factors like "I liked the wrapper" or "It looked cool," you're the type of person who makes judgments based on appearance alone. Just remember, it's the candy you eat, not the wrapper.

2. The number of children who entered the store while you shopped represents the number of people in your life you need to depend on. We all need support, whether it's actual physical assistance in the work we do or just encouragement from the people we love. You can't go through life completely on your own. But it's also true that relying too much on others makes it difficult to achieve personal autonomy.

Most people imagine between one and five children entering the store. People who said more than five children came into the store still have a way to go before they reach an adult level of independence. But those who said no children come in also might need to reconsider the way they look at the world.

3. The number of free treats you got reveals how much you still depend on your mother. The amount of special attention the storekeeper showed you is a measure of the attention you actually want from your mother. Most adults say one or two pieces. If you answered ten or twenty, you may need to think about spreading your wings a little more and flying away from the nest.

4. To whom would you give the candy? The person you chose is a person you would like to be able to take care of someday or have become dependent on you. Did you say you gave it to your parents? Your wish may be a reality sooner than you think.

Was it your partner or a person you secretly like? It might be fun taking care of them for a day or two, but that could wear thin.

Or did you say you wouldn't give the candy to anyone? You prefer a life with few attachments, asking little from the world and expecting the same in return. That solitary approach means you may never have to share with anyone, but it also means you may never have anyone to share with.

THE RIDE OF YOUR LIFE

Even for people with normally happy lives, there come times when the everyday seems just a little boring and, well, everyday. Although it's certainly nice to be able to know that tomorrow will be a good day, too much predictability can leave you uninspired. But we know a way to escape that daily routine, if only for a short while. The answer lies in seeking out stimulation and the occasional thrill. This is the secret to being able to appreciate the value of even our everyday lives.

How do we bring thrills into our lives? Watching movies, traveling, and playing sports and games of chance. Or maybe a trip to an amusement park, a world where thrills mingle with fantasies. Let's take a trip back to that realm of childhood excitement and fun.

You will need a pencil and paper for this quiz.

1. You enter the park gate, and a roller coaster looms before you with a line of people waiting their turn. How long do you have to wait in line before getting to ride?

2. Your turn finally comes and now you're racing and plunging around the course. What kinds of feelings does the speed bring out in you?

3. At the most exciting point in the course, the roller coaster dives into a pool of water and you're drenched by the spray. What do you shout or scream at this instant?

4. Next you decide to try the merry-go-round. But during your ride, for some reason the horse you're riding breaks down and stops moving. What do you say to the horse?

5. Your ride on the roller coaster was exciting, but it wasn't all that it could have been. If you were going to design the perfect roller coaster, what would the course look like? Draw a detailed picture of the course.

KEY TO THE RIDE OF YOUR LIFE

$\left(\!D\!\right)$ id you have a good time in the park? In psychological terms, rhythmical up-and-down motions represent sexual excitement. So your responses to the five questions actually show your attitudes toward sex.

1. The time you spent waiting in line reveals how much time you spend, or would like your partner to spend, on foreplay.

    Did you have to stand in line for hours before the main event, or did you just jump aboard without waiting?

2. Your feelings during the roller-coaster ride reveal how you feel while making love.

    Did you think, "This is the best ride I've ever been on!" or was your reaction closer to, "Get me off this thing! I think I'm gonna throw up!"

3. In Jungian symbolism, water represents the source of life. Your words at the moment the roller coaster splashed into the pool show what you might say at the moment of sexual climax.

    Let's hope you didn't say anything you'll end up regretting in the morning.

4. The horse, in psychosexual terms, is a symbol of the masculine principle. Your words to your broken-down steed reflect what you might say to yourself or to your partner in situations where the man failed to rise to the occasion.

"It's all right, don't worry about it. It's only a ride." You have a truly gentle and forgiving nature.

"I can't believe this. I want my money back!" You said it, not me.

"Come on you stupid animal, giddyap!" Yikes!

5. Your plan for the ideal roller-coaster course shows your vision of the perfect sex life.

The ups and downs of a roller-coaster ride are an exact metaphor for the thrills and lulls of lovemaking. Was it a long, slow ascent followed by a terrifying plunge? A series of acrobatic loop-the-loops and 360-degree rolls? Or maybe you drew a course where you spend the whole ride turned upsidedown and backward? Don't worry, your secret is safe with us.

You're Only Human

I can't believe it! How could I do something so stupid?" We have all too many chances to say those words. Burned toast, coffee stains on paperwork, sleeping through the alarm clock, stubbed toes, missed exits—it's human nature to goof up once in a while. Nobody's perfect, and each of us proves that every day. Keep that in mind the next time you're tempted to laugh at other people's careless mistakes. After all, you never know when it'll be your turn to wear mismatched socks to work.

You're walking down the street, thinking of other things, when you stumble into a garbage can on the sidewalk and knock it over. What comes spilling out from under the lid?

1. Nothing comes out—the can was empty.
2. A pile of loose trash spills out onto the street.
3. Apple cores, chicken bones, and other raw garbage.
4. A well-tied black plastic garbage bag.

KEY TO YOU'RE ONLY HUMAN

I n your carelessness you overturned a garbage can, dumping out something that had been neatly shut away and exposing it for all the world to see. Your image of the can's contents reveals things inside you that you try to hide from public view.

1. Nothing comes out—the can was empty.

People who gave this answer tend to live their lives without making displays or false pretenses. What you see is what you get. It's this simple honesty that gives them their charm.

2. A pile of loose trash spills out onto the street.

Those of you who said the can was full of loose trash may seem to be straightforward and forthright to others but actually have a pile of unexpressed feelings locked up within. You may notice these feelings only as a general sense of frustration, but when you think about it, aren't there places where you've been holding back from saying the things you really feel?

3. Apple cores, chicken bones, and other raw garbage.

People who imagined a pile of kitchen waste are suppressing their appetites and the natural desire for food. Maybe you're on (or just avoiding) a diet. Or trying to save money by cutting back on eating expenses. Whatever the case, it's taking its toll on you.

There's no need to overdo it, but it might do you good to spend a well-earned night out at a restaurant with friends.

4. A well-tied black plastic garbage bag.

People who saw a neatly tied garbage bag have a strong sense of self-control. Maybe too strong. You hate to show weakness or make complaints—your pride won't allow it. But letting others know how you really feel is no sign of weakness. Loosen up the drawstrings and let in some air before all that garbage goes bad and starts to smell.

Abracadabra, Ala-Kazam

P laying cards that dance through the air . . . rabbits produced from a silk top hat . . . a lovely assistant made to disappear in a puff of smoke. Stage magic is simple deception raised to the level of entertainment. As you watch the performance, you know you're being tricked, but no matter how hard you think about it or how closely you watch the hands, it seems you can never put your finger on the secret. But somehow the witty banter and the sleight of hand make it all fun, and you sit back and enjoy the display of baffling skill. Perhaps the most important part of the magician's act is not in the mastery of the actual techniques or the preparation of the props, but in the ability to make an audience willing to believe.

Wouldn't it be nice to have that same skill? Well, tonight is your big chance. Your audience is waiting, and the curtain is about to rise. . . .

1. You are a stage magician, just setting off on another long tour. Tonight is opening night, and you are waiting in the wings of the stage for your act to be announced. How do you feel in the moments before your show begins?

2. Part of your act involves calling a member of the audience up on stage to help you with a trick. Whom do you call to assist you? Give the name of a person you know.

3. Despite all your years of training and experience, somehow the trick goes terribly wrong. What do you say to the person you called up to participate?

4. You're back in your dressing room after your act. How do you feel now that the show has ended?

KEY TO ABRACADABRA, ALA-KAZAM

(F) eats of magic are called *tricks* for a reason. They necessarily involve making people see things that aren't really there or miss realities that are staring them in the face. Essentially, tricks involve deception and guile. And the way you pictured your own performance shows how you see yourself when it comes to lying to or deceiving others, especially the people closest to you.

1. Your feelings as you waited to go on tell us how you would feel when planning (or merely fantasizing about) an illicit affair. Most people say something like "I hope I don't mess this up" or "Wow, I'm really nervous." But then there are those who seem to be immune to performance anxiety: "I'm gonna go out there and give them a night to remember!"

2. The person you asked to join you as your helper on stage is someone you see as simple, naive, and just a little bit gullible. In short, it's someone you think is easy to deceive or lie to. If you happened to name your current partner, it would be a good idea now to reassure him or her that of course you'd never do anything like that in real life.

3. The words you said after flubbing your act reveal the types of excuses you'd make if you got caught cheating.

Did you get flustered and turn red before blurting out, "Sorry, 'bout that."

Or did you just try to laugh it off and get on with the show: "Whoopsy daisy! Well, I guess that goes to show nobody's perfect!"

Or are you of the group that tried to pretend it was just part of the act? That'd be a neat trick if you could really pull it off.

4. The way you felt after the act was finished is the way you feel after doing or saying something dishonest.

"That was nerve-racking. What a mess!" That'll teach you to go around tricking people.

"That settles it. I'm getting out of this business." There are plenty of more satisfying careers for an honest, hardworking type. You're probably not cut out for all this smoke-and-mirrors stuff anyway.

"I'll get it right next time." Some people never learn. You may want to think about getting into politics, law, or used-car sales.

"Actually, I thought the whole experience was kind of stimulating." They say that once a fox has had its first chicken, it never forgets the taste.

In the Pages of a Magazine

ou've just bought a copy of a popular weekly magazine and taken it home to read. How do you go through the features inside?

1. Read the whole magazine in order from first page to last.
2. Jump straight to the articles that you know will interest you and read only them.
3. Flip randomly through the pages and read anything that seems worthwhile.
4. As long as the format hasn't been changed, you'd read the features in the same order as you always do.

KEY TO IN THE PAGES OF A MAGAZINE

(Y) our average weekly magazine represents the collected effort of a great many writers, designers, photographers, and editors offering a spectrum of opinions and points of view. It is an omnibus of the human experience, and your magazine reading style reflects how you confront that diversity of choices. In particular, the way you budget your reading time reveals your approach to handling resources, especially money.

1. Read the whole magazine in order from first page to last.

You're the type who knows where every penny of your money is and what it's being spent on. It's not that you're all that concerned about your budget or financial planning; you just feel more comfortable when you know exactly how things stand. You hate the thought of missing something, so you keep all your accounts in order and know the current balance of your checking account, including interest, as a matter of course.

2. Jump straight to the articles that you know will interest you and read only them.

Money burns a hole in your pocket. If you have it, you use it to buy whatever catches your fancy and think, Maybe I'll start a savings account next month, as you spend your last dime. If you have managed to save something, it's not unusual for you to make a trip to the cash machine and make a withdrawal just to give you something to do.

3. Flip randomly through the pages and read anything that seems worthwhile.

You'd say you're economical. Some would call it stingy. The fact is you don't spend frivolously or waste your resources, preferring to save it for a rainy day. You'll never get carried away with impulse buying or max out your credit cards shopping on cable TV, but you might want to loosen up those purse strings on occasion. After all, money is there to help you live well.

4. As long as the format hasn't been changed, you'd read the features in the same order as you always do.

You keep spending according to habit regardless of changes that take place in your life. If you hit the lottery, it would be hard for you to stop shopping at discount stores. Alternately, if you were facing bankruptcy, you might still insist on designer label clothes. You can't be bothered worrying about the vagaries of fortune, which would make it a good idea for you to hook up with a partner who can, and let him or her handle the finances.

UNDER A CLEAR BLUE SKY

I magine a clear blue sky without a cloud in sight. Just thinking about it should give your spirits a little lift. Now turn your mind's eye down to survey the landscape. Which of the following scenes feels most calming and relaxing to you?

1. A white snowy plain.
2. A blue seascape.
3. A green mountain.
4. A field of yellow flowers.

KEY TO UNDER A CLEAR BLUE SKY

T he color blue has power to soothe the soul. Even a blue image in the mind can slow the pulse and make you take a deep breath. Other colors have significance, too. The scene you pictured contrasted against that clear blue sky reveals a hidden talent that resides in the depths of your untroubled mind.

1. A white snowy plain.

You are blessed with a special sensitivity that allows you to comprehend situations at a glance and decipher complex problems without needing any proof or explanation. You have what it takes to be a clear-sighted decision maker and even something of a visionary. Always trust your first intuitions; they will guide you well.

2. A blue seascape.

You have a natural talent for interpersonal relations. People respect your ability to communicate with others and the way you help bring diverse groups together. Just by being around, you help others work more smoothly and efficiently, making you an invaluable member of any project or team. When you say, "Nice job. Keep up the good work," people know you mean it. So it means that much more to them.

3. A green mountain.

Your gift is for expressive communication. You always seem to be able to find the words to express the way you feel, and people soon realize it's exactly how they were feeling, too. They say that joy shared is multiplied, while shared grief is divided. You always seem able to help others find the right side of that equation.

4. A field of yellow flowers.

You are a storehouse of knowledge and creativity, bursting with ideas and almost infinite potential. Keep attuned to the feelings of others and never stop working on building your dreams, and there is nothing you cannot achieve.

INTO THE DEPTHS

Every adventure involves an element of danger—it's the danger that makes adventures so exciting and hard to resist. People willingly spend good money to experience that same thrill without the physical risk. It's this fact of human nature that keeps haunted house attractions and sky-diving schools in business. The impulse to face risks is in us all. Indeed, the fascination with danger can prove to be such a powerful lure that some people will gamble with their own lives to confront a mystery or explore a new world. We've all watched as the unwitting hero of a horror movie is about to walk through a darkened doorway and wanted to yell, "Don't go in there! Are you crazy?" But what would you do if it was you?

Our next scenario leads us into that dark world, where the line between simple thrills and actual fear is blurred. . . .

1. You are in an old, abandoned building where no human has set foot for years and have discovered a staircase leading underground. Slowly you make your way down, counting the steps as you go. One step . . . two . . . three . . . How many steps is it to the bottom of the stairs?

2. The underground room is pitch black. Then, from the darkness you hear the sound of another person. Is the person weeping softly? Moaning wordlessly? Is it a voice speaking to you?

3. How do you react on hearing the sound of this other person? Do you try to search out the source? Is your first instinct to run up the stairs without looking back? Or are you paralyzed with fear and frozen where you stand?

4. You hear a person now calling your name and see a figure descending from the light at the top of the stairs. Who is this person coming down the stairs?

KEY TO INTO THE DEPTHS

$\left(\text{A}\right)$ bandoned buildings and underground rooms are highly symbolic of buried memories and old psychological scars. All of us have had an experience we'd rather not recall or a heartbreak we thought we'd forgotten. But the memory is not so easily erased, and the things we hoped to forget linger for longer than we'd like to admit. Your responses to this situation show how you deal with painful memories of the past.

1. The number of steps to the bottom of the stairs indicates the impact of the psychological scars you are bearing.

People who said there were only a few stairs feel little adverse effect from the past. But those who described a long staircase leading deep into the earth carry correspondingly deep wounds inside.

2. The sounds you heard out of the darkness reveal how you got through bad experiences in your past.

Those who said they heard weeping have been comforted by others in times of trouble and recovered with the help they received. The people who took care of you in their kindness have helped you become the person you are today. The tears you cried were not in vain.

People who heard wordless moaning went through the hard times in their past alone. The moaning you hear in the dark is your own buried pain. Perhaps the time has come to open the door and let the sun shine in. Things won't look so bleak in the light of day.

Those who heard a voice speaking to them wear their old scars like a badge of honor, refusing to think of them as wounds. Nietzsche said, "That which does not kill us, makes us stronger," and you seem to have taken this philosophy to heart. But be careful not to let this harden you to the feelings of others.

3. Your reaction to the sounds in the darkness shows how you deal with the painful aspects of your own past.

If you went out to search for the source of the sound, it's likely you show the same take-charge attitude in your own life. By facing your problems head-on, you're bound to discover solutions.

Those of you who ran straight back upstairs without confronting the sounds have a history of ignoring problems in the hopes that they'll just go away. That approach may work sometimes, but don't be surprised when trouble stays around longer than you anticipated. Sometimes you need to stand and face your fears.

If you were frozen in place with fear, it may be that you have unresolved conflicts in your own past that continue to haunt you and keep you from moving ahead with your life.

4. The person who appeared at the top of the stairs calling your name is someone you feel you can rely on in times of trouble. The name you gave is the person you believe will comfort you and help to heal your inner wounds.

IN THE BAG

All of us lose things. Sometimes we don't even realize they're lost. Think about the last time you lost something: that sense of frustration as you retraced your steps, scanning the ground, looking under furniture, and sifting through the trash. Remember the feeling of desperation as you checked your pockets for the fifth time just to make sure you didn't miss it? Lost objects have a way of staying lost, only to turn up months after you've given up looking and forgotten all about them. Finding things lost by other people works the same way. You don't find dropped wallets in the street or lost purses on the train by consciously going out to look for them. If you find one, it's usually just by stumbling across it while you're doing something else.

You're walking down the street when you come across a closed black briefcase. There's no one else around, and when you open it to check for the owner's name, out spills a bundle of cash. What is your first reaction to this sudden windfall?

1. "Hey, this must be my lucky day!"
2. "Oh no, what am I going to do now?"
3. "I'd better take a night to think this over."
4. "God must have wanted me to have this."

KEY TO IN THE BAG

$\left(\text{Y}\right)$ our reaction on finding the bag of money reveals how you would react if an attractive person suddenly asked you out on a date.

1. "Hey, this must be my lucky day!"

You have a childlike capacity for joy at your own good fortune. If more people could express their happiness like you, the world would be a better place.

2. "Oh no, what am I going to do now?"

It's normal to feel a little uncertain at times like these. But in the end the decision is all up to you. Take your time and think it over, but don't spend too long wringing your hands or someone else might just come along and snatch your good fortune out from under your nose.

3. "I'd better take a night to think this over."

Big decisions should be made with a clear head after a good night's sleep. There's a lot to be said for your policy of looking before you leap, but wouldn't it feel good every once in a while to cross the street without looking both ways? Sometimes you need to go with your instincts, even if it means taking some unacceptable risks. Love and danger go hand in hand.

4. "God must have wanted me to have this."

Either you don't take divine intervention very seriously, or you think of dating as a religious experience.

CINDERELLA STORY

The rags-to-riches story of a girl whose dreams come true, Cinderella is one of the classic fairy tales in world literature. Of all the memorable scenes in the tale, which stands out most in your mind?

1. Cinderella suffering at the hands of her wicked stepmother.
2. Cinderella being transformed into a beautiful princess by her fairy godmother.
3. Cinderella losing her slipper on the steps to the palace as the clock strikes midnight.
4. The scene where the prince finally finds her and fits the glass slipper on her foot.

KEY TO CINDERELLA STORY

(W) hy do you react so strongly to the scene you picked? A closer look at the elements of each scene tells us your choice is related to your greatest character weakness or flaw.

1. Cinderella suffering at the hands of her wicked stepmother.

The thought of poor Cinderella scrubbing the floors while her stepmother and sisters showered her with abuse evokes strong feelings of pity. But on the underside of pity lie feelings of superiority and pride. You remember this scene for the way it made you feel better than someone. It's good for you to be able to look down at others with a tender eye, but be wary of your tendency to look down on them all the time.

2. Cinderella being transformed into a beautiful princess by her fairy godmother.

With a wave of her magic wand, her fairy godmother makes Cinderella into an enchanted princess and changes her world forever. But here in the real world, things are not so easy to do. Your biggest faults are your blindness to the practical questions in life and your lack of attention to planning and consequences. You seem to forget that there are no fairy godmothers waiting to save you from the problems you create for yourself.

3. Cinderella losing her slipper on the steps to the palace as the clock strikes twelve.

This scene left a strong impression on you because it played upon your sense of dependency on others. It's easy to see yourself running out at the stroke of midnight, leaving behind nothing but problems and unanswered questions. In the short term, relying on others to clean up your messes may seem like the easy way through life, but one day you're going to have to face the music.

4. The scene where the prince finally finds her and fits the glass slipper on her foot.

Almost everybody loves a happy ending, and you count yourself among them. And therein lies your problem. You're too easily satisfied with the simple, the normal, and the average. All you expect from life is an average job, an average salary, average friends, average family, average kids . . . Work on discovering more of what makes you unique and original. Remember, you're an individual, even if you don't feel like one.

(Not So) Happily Ever After

F airy tales have happy endings. They're supposed to, anyway. But what would you do if the happy ending you were waiting for didn't turn out as expected?

Picture yourself as Cinderella, standing by as the handsome prince tries to fit your lost slipper on your wicked and ugly stepsister's foot. Then imagine seeing her ecstatic grin as her foot slides in effortlessly—a perfect fit! How would you react to this unpleasant surprise? Describe in detail how you'd feel and what you'd do about it.

KEY TO (NOT SO) HAPPILY EVER AFTER

(I) n the story, the glass slipper represents the one thing Cinderella believed to be entirely and forever hers and hers alone. When you imagined yourself in her place, you took on that same set of feelings. The way you reacted to the unpleasant surprise ending shows the way you'd respond to a rival in love who tried to steal your partner from you. We all like to think our partners belong to us completely, but there are many ways of expressing that in action. What did you do to get back what was rightfully yours?

"I'd make the prince let me try on the slipper, too." You're not afraid to let your partners shop around a little before accepting that you're the only one for them. That's admirable self-confidence, but what are you going to do when the prince decides there's a whole kingdom of feet he hasn't tried that slipper on yet?

"I'd just accept it as bad luck and get on with my life." Having patience is a sign of wisdom, but sometimes you have to fight to hold on to what belongs to you.

"I'd grab that glass slipper and crack my ugly stepsister over the head with it." It may feel good to express your natural resentment, but the prince might not think much of his future bride getting into a catfight.

UNTAMED

When you see a tiger or leopard at the zoo, you can't help feeling it looks a little tame, as though something in its wild nature has been lost. Even huge creatures like elephants or grizzly bears seem diminished when they're locked up in a cage. That may be the reason safari parks have become so popular. The impact of seeing wild animals is so much greater when you can watch them in their natural state, and the thrill is that much more when only a thin car window stands between you and a hungry lion.

You are on a safari park tour, following the road through the open savanna. A short distance from the trail, you see a lion and lioness feeding, hungrily tearing at and devouring hunks of raw meat. What are you thinking as you watch this scene of untamed savagery?

KEY TO UNTAMED

$\left(\text{A}\right)$ safari tour allows you to observe dangerous wildlife from a safe and protected distance, and the lions feeding represent a scene of natural forces unleashed. Your reaction to the scenario shows how you reacted (or would react) on seeing an adult video for the first time. What was your response?

"Wow! Look at them go! Hey, I'm getting a little hungry, too." That doesn't take much interpretation, does it?

"I don't want to watch that—it's disgusting." Nobody said it was going to be pretty.

"I'm scared." It's natural to be a little bit frightened, but you're safe as long as you stay on this side of the glass.

"Oh, give the poor things some privacy." You're truly a decent person, but are you sure you don't want to watch just a little bit longer?

MIDNIGHT CALLER

As you fall sleep, you enter what could be called another world, as far from this one as any distant star. In that remote space, even familiar voices and sounds seem alien and strange. It is a world utterly removed from the one where we spend our waking hours, a world where the mind is free to roam.

You are lying in bed in that foggy zone between consciousness and sleep when the telephone at your bedside rings. It takes a tremendous effort to reach out for the receiver, almost as if you were moving underwater. You fumble to get the right ends aligned with your mouth and ear and manage to mumble, "Hello?" Who is the voice on the other end of the line, and what does that person say to you?

KEY TO MIDNIGHT CALLER

B eing awakened suddenly from a slumber is disorienting and sometimes a little bit scary. It's a natural instinct to turn to others for help when you're confused or afraid. So although the ringing phone is the cause of your confusion, the voice you hear on the line is actually someone you depend on in difficult times.

Whom did you name, and what words of reassurance did they offer you?

Was it a familiar voice saying, "Hello? It's your mother. How come you never call me?" Well, you can always depend on mothers for that.

Or was it just a friend calling to talk for no special reason? Sometimes that's the best kind of reassurance when you're feeling scared.

WHALE WATCHING

You are standing on the deck of a small whale-watching boat. The great blue ocean surrounds you on all sides as far as the eye can see. The salt spray mists your face as you lean over the rail to try to catch sight of these mysterious creatures of the deep. And then there they are—a family of whales has surfaced just a short distance away!

Which of the following best describes the family?

1. A small baby whale swimming behind its gigantic mother.
2. A baby whale snuggling close to its mother's belly.
3. A father and mother whale swimming with their baby.
4. A baby whale blowing a water spout as it swims off alone.

KEY TO WHALE WATCHING

(T) he whale is a common instance of Jung's "Great Mother" archetype. The relationship you imagined between the whales in this scene is linked to the feelings you have about your own relationship with your mother.

1. A small baby whale swimming behind its gigantic mother.

The role of the mother is almost overwhelmingly important to you. It may be that your own mother is influencing the way you act and think even now that you're an adult. It might be a good idea to cut away some of those apron strings and work toward a new level of independence. After all, your mother didn't raise you to be a child forever.

2. A baby whale snuggling close to its mother's belly.

You crave physical affection. It's natural and normal to feel the need for human warmth, but you feel that need more than others. Men who gave this answer should be especially careful not to look to their partners to play the role of the surrogate mother—playing Mommy's little boy is no way to run a mature romance.

3. A father and mother whale swimming with their baby.

You have an equal appreciation for the roles of both your mother and your father (the father is often forgotten about in these types of imaginary scenes). As a child, your home life was most likely happy and secure, and the result is your balanced outlook on life.

4. A baby whale blowing a waterspout as it swims off alone.

You have achieved personal autonomy and are well on your way to real growth as an individual, but your insistence on being your own person can sometimes make you appear to be willful, headstrong, or just plain selfish. Take care not to be so individualistic that you alienate the people around you.

BLOWING YOUR OWN HORN

Humans aren't the only entertainers in the animal kingdom. We've all watched the horse shows in a circus, the tumbling bears, and the antics of chimpanzees on tricycles. Then there are the star performers of the watery world—dolphins, killer whales, and, let's not forget, the seals.

You are a seal in a marine park show, performing in front of a sellout crowd. What runs through your mind as you face out into the audience, pumping your horns and waiting for the next bucket of fish from your trainer?

KEY TO BLOWING YOUR OWN HORN

(T) rained animals performing in a show are doing a kind of forced labor, with no option of quitting midway. The thoughts you said went through your head on stage correspond to the feelings you have about your own job. The things you said to yourself are things you're really thinking while you're at work. What did you have to say?

"Can you believe these idiots are actually paying to see this?" You'd be surprised what the entertainment value of your efforts is to an outside observer.

"Hey, buddy, how about some salmon next time? If I have to eat another sardine, I think I'm gonna puke." Rephrase that sentiment and tell it to your boss the next time you're up for a salary review. The squeaky wheel gets the grease.

"This is so humiliating. I can't believe I'm doing this where all these people can see me." What was it you said you do again? Maybe you should look into a nice relaxing job in accounting.

PLANTING THE SEEDS

he human spirit loves a challenge. This desire to overcome may be the secret to our success as a species. Every human science was born through hard study and failed experiments; and every human personality is the product of an innate drive to create something unique from one's raw individual experience. The need to be challenged is so strong in us that we sometimes make things more difficult than they need to be, just so we can rise to the occasion and overcome the obstacles we have ourselves created.

You are an eminent scientist who has been working to develop a new species of plant. You have spent years in your laboratory experimenting, and now your efforts have begun to show results. As the ultimate test of the hardiness of your creation, you plant 100 seeds of the new strain in an inhospitable desert location.

How many of those 100 seeds sprout? (Give a number from 0 to 100.)

KEY TO PLANTING THE SEEDS

T he number you gave as an answer correlates to your self-confidence level. In this story, the scientist stands for feelings of confidence and even pride. On the other hand, the hostile desert sands represent a difficult challenge or test and therefore elicit feelings of doubt and uncertainty. People who answered with higher numbers felt greater affinity with the scientist and have high confidence levels. Those who answered with lower numbers felt the challenge was too great and have correspondingly lower self-confidence.

Scale

99–100. It's an understatement to say you're self-confident; maybe a better word would be "vain." Sure, it's important to believe in yourself, but you tend to dismiss the challenges of the rest of the world. Don't forget that one of the truest signs of strength is accepting one's own weaknesses.

81–98. You radiate confidence in yourself and your own capabilities, but somehow it doesn't come across as arrogance. Those around you generally feel it as a sense of cool certainty, making you a natural leader wherever you go.

61–80. Maybe you're best described as a cautious optimist, hoping for the best but always prepared for the worst. That realistic philosophy keeps you grounded when others might lose their heads in the clouds.

41–60. Your self-confidence is in the average range—neither too cocky nor too unsure. Maybe you're still finding out what it is you're best at, or maybe you just have a healthy respect for the difficulties that stand before you. Believe in yourself and the world will follow suit.

21–40. While you don't doubt yourself entirely, you tend to overestimate the challenges confronting you. You may excuse this tendency as a simple resignation to the facts, but your pessimistic outlook affects the way other people see you. The only way for you to inspire confidence in others is first to have it in yourself.

1–20. It's one thing to be humble, but you need to focus on developing a better sense of your own value. There's nothing wrong with believing you can achieve great things, and with a little hard work you can. The only thing holding you back is you.

0. What looks like an utter lack of confidence is actually a sign of perfectionistic pride. You can't tolerate the thought of being proven wrong or even making a mistake, so you pretend that everything is too difficult for you. If you don't learn to face those fears, you may fool the world into thinking you're just a ne'er-do-well, but you'll always know that you never even tried.

THE STOLEN BERRIES

E veryone likes a nice person, and most of us try to be good in our own lives. Why is it, then, that there are so few people in the world who are good all the time? As hard as you may try, there are always those rotten days and moments of weakness where it just feels better to be bad. Whether that takes the form of driving too fast on the highway, cheating on a test, or "liberating" a box of pens from the office, we've all done things we can't be proud of or justify. The key to becoming a truly good person is in accepting the bad parts of your own personality and admitting that you're not perfect, not in trying to act like a saint while the devil on your shoulder whispers in your ear. We all succumb to temptation sometimes. But in the next scenario you might just get caught. . . .

1. On a stroll through the countryside, you come across a field of delicious-looking strawberries. Your stomach starts to rumble, and there's no one else around. Only a fence stands between you and a free lunch. How high is that fence?

2. You sneak into the garden and begin to help yourself to the fruit. How many berries do you eat?

3. Suddenly the farmer whose berries you're stealing appears out of nowhere and starts yelling at you. What do you say in your own defense?

4. After all is said and done, how did the berries taste? And looking back, how did you feel after your berry-stealing adventure was over?

KEY TO THE STOLEN BERRIES

S trawberries—seductively juicy and red—are a common symbol of sexual attraction and desire. The way you envisioned this scenario helps us to understand your attitude toward forbidden romance and stolen love.

1. The height of the fence you imagined around the field is a measure of your own level of self-control and resistance to sexual temptation. The higher the fence, the greater your own defenses. People who imagined a total enclosure exercise admirable restraint. Those of you who said it was only a string tied around some beanpoles at about knee height run a higher than average risk of getting burned by the flames of love.

2. The number of berries you said you would steal is the number of people you can believe yourself in love (or lust) with at any given time. If you said you'd quit after eating just one, you're likely to be faithful in your own love life as well (or at least a devoted serial monogamist). Those of you who got into the double digits may need to think seriously about applying the brakes on your libido. Nobody can keep that pace up forever.

3. The excuses you made to the farmer represent the way you'd defend yourself if you got caught having an affair. What was your excuse?

"I'm so sorry. I promise I'll never do it again." Sometimes a full confession and a promise to behave is the best way to get yourself off the hook.

"They looked so good, I just couldn't help myself." Well, actually you did help yourself—to somebody else's berries. But honesty is the best policy. After all, it worked for George Washington, didn't it? If you keep it up, maybe someday you could be president, too.

"Hey those berries were great! Do you mind if I have a couple more?" Farmers have shotguns. Spouses have lawyers. Fortunately you still have a chance to reconsider your choice of words.

4. The way you described the experience and the taste of the berries gives an indication of how you imagine yourself feeling when looking back on a past affair.

"Actually, they didn't taste as good as they looked. The whole thing wasn't really even worth the effort." All too true for most affairs. Chalk it up to experience and put it behind you.

"So sweet! So juicy and delicious! I've never tasted anything like it!" Uh, let's just say you're addicted to love.

"The berries were nothing special, but all in all it was kind of fun." Statistically speaking, you're in the high-risk group for repeat offenders.

CAUGHT IN THE RAIN

Not everything in life is predictable. We're always getting hit by surprises, emergencies, and unforeseen disasters without any chance to prepare ourselves mentally. Surprises of any kind can be stressful—an unexpected proposal just as much as a sudden breakup. There are too many things we can't predict or control; that's one of the reasons we all tend to develop habits and patterns to live by.

You are walking outside when a hard rain suddenly begins to fall. Even if you run full speed, you're still about five minutes from your destination. Which of the following best describes your choice of action?

1. "I'd find an awning or tree to stand under and wait for the rain to stop."

2. "I don't know how long it's going to keep raining, so I'd run to where I'm going as fast as I could."

3. "I'd see if there was anybody around with an umbrella I could share or a store where I could buy one."

4. "I always have a folding umbrella in my bag when I go out, so I'd just use that."

KEY TO CAUGHT IN THE RAIN

(H) ow did you respond to the sudden downpour? The rainstorm represents unforeseeable and uncontrollable forces in life. Specifically, your answer shows how you tend to react when a fight breaks out between you and a loved one or friend.

1. "I'd find an awning or tree to stand under and wait for the rain to stop."

You're the type who waits for the other side in a fight to cool off before trying to settle your differences. You prefer to let them rant and rave until they run out of steam, then present your case calmly and objectively. Some would say this is the intelligent approach, others would say it's just sneaky.

2. "I don't know how long it's going to keep raining, so I'd run to where I'm going as fast as I could."

You don't care about the end result of a fight so much as getting to speak your mind. You're sure you're right, and there's no sense in arguing the point. The concept of give-and-take doesn't figure into your tactics. If they get angry, you get angrier. If they start to yell, you scream. This doesn't make you much fun to argue with, but at least it's easy to tell where you stand on an issue.

3. "I'd see if there was anybody around with an umbrella I could share or a store where I could buy one."

You don't like conflicts and confrontations, so you try to smooth things over and calm the other person down whenever a fight breaks out. Unfortunately, sometimes that only makes things worse. It may be important for you to make a stand and weather the storm every once in a while.

4. "I always have a foldable umbrella in my bag when I go out, so I'd just use that."

You think you have an answer for every accusation, a justification for every fault. To you, an argument may be just a chance to hone your skills at debate, but to others you seem slippery, frustrating, and insincere. But of course, you probably have a good explanation for that, too.

ADRIFT ON THE BREEZE

Can you still remember those long summer days when school was out, you had no responsibilities, and there was nothing but time from when you woke up till the sun finally went down? Time for play and adventure, time to daydream and roam. Hours to spend on childhood diversions . . . flying kites . . . watching clouds . . . blowing bubbles . . .

Imagine you are out again on a childhood summer's day, blowing bubbles in an open field. Which of the following best describes the scene you imagined?

1. The bubbles you blow float away high into the sky.
2. You are blowing hundreds of tiny bubbles through your plastic ring.
3. You're concentrating on blowing a single enormous bubble.
4. The bubbles you make are carried behind you on the breeze.

KEY TO ADRIFT ON THE BREEZE

(T) he shimmering bubbles you blow in your imagination are symbols of your hopes and dreams. The scene you described reveals how you think about the dreams you hope someday will come true.

1. The bubbles you blow float away high into the sky.

You see your own dreams as elusive and unattainable, flying away from you like soap bubbles on the wind. Maybe you're wishing for too much, too soon or are caught up in an impossible fantasy. Whatever the case may be, the gap between your dreams and reality is wide. As much as you may like to tell others of your grand schemes and plans for the future, somewhere inside yourself is a voice telling you just how fragile and fleeting those dreams are.

2. You are blowing hundreds of tiny bubbles through your plastic ring.

You've set your sights on the immediate attainables—new clothes, a car, a boyfriend or girlfriend. Your dreams are sensible and always within your reach. Decide what it is you want most in the world and work for it. If you chase after everything at once, you stand a good chance of ending up empty-handed.

3. You're concentrating on blowing a single enormous bubble.

You have a single, all-important dream or ambition that drives your entire life. Hold on to that desire and keep striving toward your goal. Given time, you'll see that it's not so far from your grasp.

4. The bubbles you make are blown behind you on the breeze.

Your disappointing experience with unfulfilled hopes and dreams in the past shapes how you think today. But the experience of chasing after and losing a few dreams along the way was all just training for you as you make new goals for the future. Don't be afraid to keep dreaming—the only people who never fail are those who never try.

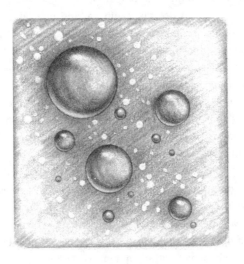

BARE NECESSITIES

There are a few common items that people keep in their pockets or a bag nearly every time they leave the house: wallet, keys, ID, and credit cards. The insides of our bags are like the insides of our heads; we all carry around a lot of the same stuff, but there's always something in each one that makes every bag unique.

You're getting ready for the day and putting together your things. Besides the bare necessities, which one of the following items do you want to take along with you?

1. Your personal organizer or address book.
2. Hairspray or mousse.
3. A lucky charm.
4. Candy or gum.

KEY TO BARE NECESSITIES

W hat is it you always want to have close at hand? The item you wanted to bring along is something you feel a little uncomfortable being without, and your choice actually tells us something about a part of your personality you feel insecure about.

1. Your personal organizer or address book.

You can't trust your memory. Phone numbers, birthdays, appointments; they run through your head like water through a sieve. You don't mean to forget things, but somehow they just never seem to stick, and you end up apologizing for missing your anniversary—again. It's probably a good idea for you to keep that address book with you all the time. Now if you could just remember where you left it.

2. Hairspray or mousse.

Appearances are all-important to you. That attention to detail means you always look great and ready to take on the world, but sometimes you take things too far. Remember, a bad hair day is not a valid excuse for calling in sick.

3. A lucky charm.

You're a firm believer in your own bad luck. The lines at the other tollbooths are always moving faster, your toast always lands jelly side down. Things never seem to go your way, and you've noticed. How couldn't you? It's not to say that you're superstitious, but you do feel a little more comfortable with your personal good-luck charm, whether it's a four-leaf clover, a St. Anthony's medal, or just a pair of old socks you've grown attached to.

4. Candy or gum.

You're worried about controlling your diet. Eating a pint of cookies 'n cream the day after starting a new diet, opening the door of the fridge every time you go past, "just to check"—your appetite fills your mind more than it does your stomach. Keeping some mints or a candy bar with you makes you feel safe. No matter what may happen over the course of the day, at least you know you won't starve to death.

SOMETHING'S FISHY

When it comes to relaxing in the great outdoors, few activities have the perennial appeal of fishing. Every weekend, no matter the weather, dedicated anglers set off for their favorite spots, joined by curious first-timers in their pursuit of the day's catch. Not many pastimes can boast the number of confirmed addicts that fishing has. What could be the secret of its allure?

You are out for a day of fishing when you get a strike. As you reel the fish up out of the water, it thrashes on the line and smacks into you. What area of your body does the fish hit?

KEY TO SOMETHING'S FISHY

(T) he fish you hooked acted out what could be interpreted as a final counterattack, and the place you imagined it striking is a part of yourself you particularly want to protect. It is a truth of human psychology that we often fantasize that those things we want to keep hidden will get found and the things we want to protect will come under attack. So the body part you named is actually a place you feel insecure or sensitive about.

Was it your face? Take a good look in the mirror. Maybe you just need to smile more.

Your stomach? Maybe your unconscious is telling you it's about time to cut down on the cheesecake.

Somewhere between the legs? Well, we all feel a little sensitive down there.

WELCOME TO MY PARLOR

I n the human unconscious, spiders hold a place of fear and respect that's entirely out of proportion to their tiny size. Perhaps it's their skill in hunting, their patience when lying in wait, or their ability to weave devious webs to trap their prey. Whatever the reason, spiders evoke a strong mixture of feelings in us all.

Imagine you are a spider, sitting at the center of a large web you have spun. ·

You will need a pencil and paper for this quiz.

1. Draw a picture of your web and the number and types of insects you have trapped in it.

2. You move to make a meal of one of your pray, but somehow it frees itself from the web and escapes. As it hurries out of reach, the lucky bug says something to you. What are its parting words?

KEY TO WELCOME TO MY PARLOR

(T)he spider is one of the great hunters of the natural world. Your impressions of life as a spider show us something about how you see your experience as a hunter in the wilds of love.

1. The number and types of bugs you drew corresponds to your own love conquests. The web represents your strategies and techniques for luring others into your clutches, while the types of bugs you caught reflect your opinion of your former lovers. Was it a single common housefly? A lovely butterfly that only leaves you hungry afterward? Perhaps a fat, juicy caterpillar? Or maybe an unappetizing mass of mosquitoes, roaches, and worms wriggling as they await your approach? Some spiders will eat anything.

2. The parting words of the bug that got away are your memories of rejection in a failed conquest. Let's face it, we've all been shot down at one time or another—this game shows the words that hit closest to home.

"You'll never catch me, you ugly old spider!" Ouch.

"Better luck next time!" Well, thanks for the encouragement, anyway.

"Hooray! I'm free, I'm free!" Okay, you're free. But you don't have to be quite so happy about it, do you?

YOU BE THE JUDGE

T he bang of the gavel, the slick attorneys matching wits, the hush that descends as the verdict is read—there are few movie settings more dramatic than a courtroom. It's a suspense-filled battle of intellects in which the line between right and wrong is often blurred and the link between law and justice can get lost in the scuffle.

If you were an actor playing in a courtroom drama, which of the following characters would you see yourself portraying?

1. The lawyer.
2. The detective.
3. The accused.
4. The witness.

KEY TO YOU BE THE JUDGE

I n psychological terms, the actor is associated with your so-cial persona (Latin for "mask"), the face you put on to deal with the outside world. Imagining yourself as an actor gives you the freedom to play the role as you truly see yourself. And the courtroom setting adds a sense of intensity and excitement to the scene. The role you saw yourself playing shows how you typically respond to a crisis situation.

1. The lawyer.

You normally keep your cool under fire and rarely let others see you sweat. But you also have a different face that surfaces only under the most intense pressure—a hotheaded fighter who's able to forget restraint and explode when the case demands it. This com-bination of cool readiness and fiery passion carries you through even the most desperate situations.

2. The detective.

You don't get swept away by chaos and confusion and always keep your head while others around you lose theirs. People sense and respect that imperturbability and tend to turn to you for help when they're in distress. This means that trouble seems to follow you, but you don't mind the added stress—in fact, it only makes you calmer.

3. The accused.

At first glance you seem tough and unconcerned, but underneath, you lack what it takes to see your battles through to the end. When things get tough, you waste time second-guessing and judging yourself instead of addressing the problems at hand. It's probably in your own best interest to ally yourself with someone who handles things more practically.

4. The witness.

You may look cooperative and helpful in any given situation, but your flexibility and eagerness to please also make you a source of another kind of trouble. By trying to get along with everyone all the time, you end up being inconsistent and even a little untrustworthy. Don't worry so much about whether your statements are making people happy or upset. The only thing you really have to prove is yourself.

WHISPERS IN THE DARKNESS

W hen you think of a bat, the first images that spring to mind are probably dark caves, night skies, and blood-sucking monsters. But although they're an object of many fears and superstitions, bats have another secret side. Despite their wings, they are mammals like us and nurse their young with caring and affection. And though they look fierce, the society of bats is more peaceful than our own. So the next time you see a bat flitting overhead, think that it may be looking down with the same fascination and dread that you feel.

You are lost in a deep cavern, wandering through a vast network of winding passages. As you search for the way back to the surface, a bat flies up and whispers something in your ear. . . . Which of the following does the mysterious creature say?

1. "I know where the exit is."
2. "Let me show you the way out."
3. "Keep looking."
4. "You're never, ever going to get out of here."

KEY TO WHISPERS IN THE DARKNESS

n this scenario the magical bat serves as a symbol of guidance and aid for those lost and struggling. By imagining what the bat might say to you, you give an important glimpse at the way you yourself respond to others in need of your assistance.

1. "I know where the exit is."

You tend to be something of a busybody and a know-it-all. There's no question that you're always willing to lend a hand or a bit of advice, but you sometimes try to help when it's not needed, and end up looking like a meddler.

2. "Let me show you the way out."

Your big heart and selflessness serve as a shining example for others. People sense your strength and caring and are comforted just knowing you're around when a problem arises.

3. "Keep looking."

You keep your distance out of respect for other people's space. It's not that you're unhelpful, but you only give the absolute minimum when asked for advice and generally encourage people to work things out on their own. And that principle of noninterference may be the best long-term approach in helping others find their way to maturity and independence.

4. "You're never, ever going to get out of here."

When you see somebody who's down, your first impulse is to kick. It may be natural to feel a certain pleasure at other people's misfortunes, but that doesn't make it good. Your attitude isn't going to win you many friends or help you keep the ones you have. Watch out.

THE BIG BLOWUP

An erupting volcano is one of the most awesome displays of nature's fury, belching forth hot lava and poisonous smoke that can reduce the surrounding landscape to gray ash. The destruction it brings overwhelms everything in its path, and it's easy to understand how ancient civilizations could have regarded volcanoes as signs of the anger of the gods. Even today volcanoes seem to be sending us a not so subtle message about our place in the grand scheme of things.

You are standing within view of an erupting volcano. Which of the following best describes your thoughts at watching the spectacle?

1. "Maybe this is nature's way of warning us to stop destroying the earth."
2. "I guess the pressure just got too high inside there."
3. "Wow—what a sight! I'm impressed!"
4. "It's in the nature of these things to blow up. Big deal."

KEY TO THE BIG BLOWUP

(T) he thoughts you had about the volcano are linked to the way you react to explosive power, specifically the anger of a superior. We've all run into a boss, teacher, coach, or parent who throws the occasional tantrum—this scenario shows how you deal with those blowups.

1. "Maybe this is nature's way of warning us to stop destroying the earth."

You recognize when you're responsible for other people's anger and are willing to accept the blame. That same sensitivity and adult attitude lets you clear up any problems you might have caused.

2. "I guess the pressure just got too high inside there."

You place the blame for any problem squarely on someone else's shoulders. After all, if you thought you were doing something wrong, you wouldn't have done it in the first place, right?

3. "Wow—what a sight! I'm really impressed!"

You accept criticism and even outbursts in a positive way, but that's not to say you take them lightly. That sunny outlook is sure to make a favorable impression on superiors in the long run, after they've forgotten whatever it was they were yelling for.

4. "It's in the nature of these things to blow up. Big deal."

Strong words, tirades, and harsh critiques leave you unimpressed, probably because you don't listen to them. Sure, that's a low-stress to get through a chewing-out, but you're running the risk of never learning from your own mistakes. Maybe you should start paying a little more attention to all that sound and fury; it might be signifying something after all.

In Business for Yourself

T he crowded walks at a summer fair are lined with street vendors hawking their wares from tents and stands. Table after table of wooden children's toys, crafts, oil paintings, silver jewelry, and other treasures draw the eyes of passersby and make them pause a while to browse. Everything is made by hand, and no two items are alike, giving a sense of hope that a once-in-a-lifetime find waits unnoticed at the back of some counter display. The quality of the goods ranges from merely competent to exquisite craftsmanship equal to that found in the finest boutiques, and the vendors themselves, with their colorful personalities and appearances, add a dimension to the adventure that can't be found in any window-shopping experience. The scene has been set; why not stop a while and see what's up for sale?

1. You have opened a tabletop stand to sell your own original handmade jewelry. How many different types of accessories and bangles do you put on display?

2. A person walks up and looks over your table but after only a moment walks away without buying anything. What do you think to yourself?

3. Another potential customer comes up and seems extremely interested in one of your designs. In fact, you consider it the best

piece in your collection. What type of salesmanship do you use to recommend it?

4. It's time to close up shop for the day. How would you describe your sales?

KEY TO IN BUSINESS FOR YOURSELF

(F) ashion accessories like jewelry express the social side of the self. Items you make by hand only deepen that personal meaning and significance. Your responses to this scenario therefore show how you hope to be viewed by others.

1. The number of different kinds of jewelry you sell corresponds to the number of different personas or social masks you wear in different situations. These are the faces you put on in front of your friends, your parents, your boss, your partner. The more you have, the more complicated your social life will seem.

2. The feeling you had at losing a customer corresponds to your feelings after a heartbreak or other rejection. Did you feel it was something you did wrong ("I wonder what it was they didn't like?"), shrug it off and get on with your business ("No problem, there's plenty of other people in the park"), or take the chance to make some critical observations of your own ("They wouldn't know quality workmanship if it walked up and bit them on the nose!")?

3. The way you talked about your finest piece reflects what you feel your own strong points to be and the ways you try to express them to others. Did you take a low-key approach and let customers make up their own minds, hammer the point home by badgering them

incessantly, or offer to lower your asking price? Be careful not to sell yourself short.

4. Your sales total for the day is an evaluation of your own social achievement. Those who said they sold out their entire stock are not short on self-assurance. Just try not to scare people off with your boldness. If you said you had a bad day, you may need a little boost of self-esteem. Don't be too hard on yourself; customers can smell doubt a mile away. If you had average sales for the day, you're the type who understands your true place in the world without undervaluing your own worth. And that may be the key to achieving long-term success in this line of work.

BEFORE THEY HATCH

For most people, the word *egg* means a chicken's egg, and that means one thing: food. Scrambled, poached, or sunnyside up, mixed into cake batter, or gulped down raw—the variations are endless. Although we see eggs almost every day, there's something mysterious about them. Maybe it's the way they contain so much without having any seams or openings. Or maybe it's the promise of gold hidden within a plain white shell. Whatever it is—there's more to eggs than meets the eye.

Imagine an egg on a table in front of you. The egg may be of any shape, color, size, or species. You crack it open. What kind of egg is it?

1. A snake's egg.
2. A turtle's egg.
3. A dinosaur's egg.
4. A chicken's egg.

KEY TO BEFORE THEY HATCH

I n addition to being an excellent source of protein, the egg is also a symbol of future generations and your own children. The type of egg you picked holds a special meaning about the hopes and wishes you have for your own children.

1. A snake's egg.

The serpent is symbolic of both wisdom and hidden wealth, which are the very things you want your children to have most. Keep a balanced perspective and remember that what your kids will want most from you is simply love.

2. A turtle's egg.

The turtle is universally seen as a symbol of health and longevity. Your main wish for your children is good health and physical wellness.

3. A dinosaur's egg.

The thing you most want is for your children to grow into unique individuals. You don't want them to be forced into the cookie-cutter molds of school, work, and society in general. They're bound to make mistakes; you just hope they make original ones. It's an admirable goal to have for your children, but keep in mind that one of the first steps children make toward independence is rebelling against their parents.

4. A chicken's egg.

You don't have any wild dreams or ambitions for your kids. If they're happy, what else really matters? The security and simple pleasures of a normal life will do. Just one word of practical advice: There's nothing wrong with having big dreams.

HUNG OUT TO DRY

I t may seem a little old-fashioned now, but it wasn't that long ago that hanging your clothes out on a line was the only way to get them dry. Now we're blessed with automatic dryers and wash-and-wear shirts, but it used to be you had to keep an eye on the weather when you were doing your laundry or face spending a day walking around in damp jeans.

You are back in the era when everything was washed by hand and hung out to dry. The dirty clothes have started to pile up, and you really need to do the laundry today. But when you look at the sky, you see dark clouds threatening rain. What goes through your mind?

1. "Oh no, you've got to be kidding! You mean I've got to wait till tomorrow? What am I going to wear?"
2. "Let's wait for a little while and see if the weather clears up."
3. "Well, I guess I won't have to do laundry today after all."
4. "I'm going to do this damn laundry whether it rains or not."

KEY TO HUNG OUT TO DRY

(W)hen you add unexpected bad weather to the drudgery of household chores, you get a perfect example of the kinds of little stresses we face in our everyday lives. Your answer to this bad laundry day is a meter reading of the stress level you feel in your own life.

1. "Oh, no, you've got to be kidding! You mean I've got to wait till tomorrow? What am I going to wear?"

Stress level: 80. You've been letting all the little things that can and do go wrong in life get to you, and now the stress has built up so much that even the smallest annoyance can send you into a funk all day. It's time for you to take a break and relax before it starts affecting your health.

2. "Let's wait for a little while and see if the weather clears up."

Stress level: 50. You aren't overwhelmed by stress in your life, and you manage to keep a good perspective when things don't go as planned. Keep working on those problems you can solve as they arise, and you'll be fine. Remember, not all stress is bad. Let the stress in your life motivate you.

3. "Well, I guess I won't have to do laundry today after all."

Stress level: nearly 0. You don't let small problems bother you and don't see the point in worrying. You may be on to something with your easygoing philosophy; you can't stop the rain by worrying about it.

4. "I'm going to do this damn laundry whether it rains or not."

Stress level: close to 100. You feel so much stress in your life that you ignore reality and try to achieve the impossible. And when you fail, you end up with bigger problems and more stress than before. If you'd just take the time to relax and think things through, you'd see how much effort you've been wasting. Slow down and take things easier. It won't kill you to wear that same pair of socks one more day.

LIKE A MONKEY IN A CAGE

They say that the eyes are the windows to the soul, and that is true of animals as well as man. When you look into the eyes of a friendly dog, it seems to be begging you to play, while if you stare into the eyes of a cat, it looks back with cool indifference. Animals have feelings and personalities just like humans, and if we would only heed our eyes, we'd see how close our worlds really are.

You are strolling through a zoo, watching the animals in their cages. You stop in front of a single monkey in its cage and your eyes meet. The expression in its eyes seems to be communicating something. What is the monkey trying to tell you?

KEY TO LIKE A MONKEY IN A CAGE

(C) aged animals are mentally associated with the loss of freedom and the restraints placed on our natural instincts by society. And because they are humanlike in so many ways, it is particularly easy for us to empathize and identify with monkeys. The message the monkey was sending corresponds to your true feelings about the restrictions on your freedom. Specifically, they are words you'd like, but are unable, to say about a company, a group, or a social system that you feel is running your life. Do any of these answers sound familiar?

"Boy, I'd like a banana." You are easily pleased and, therefore, easily controlled. Hold out for more and you might be surprised at how much you're worth to others. Who knows, you might even get two bananas.

"All right, move along, nothing to see here." It's not the pressure of conforming to society's rules that gets to you so much as it is the lack of privacy. Don't be afraid to go off by yourself to be alone with your thoughts from time to time. You're only a single monkey; the zoo will survive for a while without you.

"I think I'm going crazy in this cage. Get me outta here!" As a licensed Kokologist, I'm prescribing you a long vacation on a nice quiet island. Take it.

THE GREATEST MYSTERY

Nobody really likes to dwell on the subject, but take just a moment now to think about what happens to us after we die. Does the soul move on to another world, or is death the absolute and final extinction of the self? Do you believe in heaven and hell or that the soul is reborn in a new body on earth? People have been wondering about these same questions for thousands of years, but in the end we have to admit that we just don't know. In this life, death remains the greatest mystery of all.

In this scenario, imagine that the soul survives after death. What form do you imagine it takes once it is freed from the body?

1. The soul is the same size and shape as its body was in life.
2. The soul retains its human form but expands in size.
3. The soul is tiny and human shaped, like a fairy.
4. The soul is like a ball of flame or a cloud, without definite form.

KEY TO THE GREATEST MYSTERY

(T) he image you have of the soul is a direct reflection of your own self-image. The nature of the soul you pictured shows how you feel about yourself.

1. The soul is the same size and shape as its body was in life.

You have one of the most valuable things in the world—self-esteem. You accept yourself, faults and all, and love yourself for what you are. Always keep that same attitude as you go through life, and keep discovering how much about you there is to love.

2. The soul retains its human form but expands in size.

You are not satisfied with yourself as things stand today. You feel there are so many things you've yet to experience and achieve, which makes you see the true self as much bigger than it is now. That dissatisfaction can be a source of inspiration if you learn to control it. Otherwise it will only haunt you as a sense of incompleteness.

3. The soul is tiny and human shaped, like a fairy.

Despite all your good qualities, you still have not discovered what it is within you that makes you great. It's not so much a feeling of dissatisfaction as it is of self-doubt. You tend to wonder, "What's wrong with me?" but you never seem to be able to put your finger on the answer. What's wrong with you is you're human, just like the rest of us, and that means imperfect. Accept that, and you'll begin to see that being human has its good points, too.

4. The soul is like a ball of flame or a cloud, without definite form.

You aren't upset by your shortcomings or proud of your strengths, and you can't be bothered in comparing yourself with others. In fact, you aren't very interested in issues of the self at all. That may be because you're incredibly shallow or because you're profoundly wise. But even that doesn't seem very important to you.

A TRUE ADVENTURE

Have you ever had a true adventure, the kind you read about in novels or watch on the silver screen? An action-filled series of cliff-hanging scrapes and brushes with destiny, and of course a touch of romance to keep interest levels high? Wouldn't you like to?

1. You are a warrior in an ancient kingdom and have been chosen to accompany the most famous hero in the land on a mission to recover a stolen treasure. What does the hero say to you as you prepare to embark on your quest?

2. Before you set off, the king summons you and gives you a sword to see you through your adventure. What kind of sword is it? Describe it in detail.

3. Your travels take you over high mountains and through dense old forests, and you encounter many obstacles and crises along the way. Now you have finally arrived at the mouth of the cave where the stolen treasure lies waiting. How many enemies have you met thus far in the course of your adventure?

4. You enter the cavern and finally discover the treasure you have been seeking. At that moment, what expression crosses the face of

the great hero you accompanied on this quest? Describe the expression in detail.

KEY TO A TRUE ADVENTURE

(B) y entering the role of a warrior charged with a mission of great importance, you also assumed the associated feelings of pride in being trusted with such responsibility. Your answers to this quiz are linked to how you handle your own pride.

1. The words the venerated hero spoke to you are words that play on your pride. In a sense, the words you imagined the hero saying are words you have a weak spot for and that can spur you to action.

Did you hear something inspiring like "Trust me," "I'm counting on you," or "We're going to have to work together"? Each has its own special significance for the way you want to be called on for help.

Or was the hero something less than encouraging—"Just stay out of the way" or "If you're thinking about quitting, now's the time"? You have a soft spot in your heart for people with cold attitudes.

2. The sword the king gave you is a symbol of your own self-pride. Was it a finely crafted shining blade or a rusty, old, barely serviceable tool?

3. The number of enemies you encountered signifies the number of obstacles and crises you see yourself as having overcome in your own life so far. The greater the number, the greater your confi-

dence in your own abilities and pride in yourself should be. How many did you say?

Several hundred? One thing you don't lack is self-assurance. Of course, after all those adventures we're sure you have very valid reasons.

Just one or two? You don't see yourself as much of an adventurer, do you? Maybe you need some more life experience to help you gain confidence in yourself.

You didn't meet any enemies? Either the villains were too scared to show their faces after hearing you were coming, or you just figured they wouldn't bother with someone insignificant like you.

4. How did the hero react on recovering the lost treasure? The great hero who led you on this adventure actually represents those characteristics you admire most in the opposite sex (regardless of the gender you imagined the hero to be). The expression you pictured on the hero's face is the expression you find most attractive on a person of the opposite sex. Was it an ear-to-ear grin? A look of proud satisfaction or plain relief? Of maybe tears of joy? Whatever the expression, remember it. Someday someone may use it to unlock your heart.

MONSTER!

Monster! We all use the word, but who among us has ever seen one? Ask a hundred people to draw a monster and they'll paint you a hundred very different pictures. There are all kinds of monsters—the ones we see in movies, those that chase us through our dreams, the monsters of fairy tales, ghost stories, and even video games. They range from three-hundred-foot lizards to monsters in human form. What image does the word conjure up for you?

A monster is stalking the landscape, terrifying and unstoppable, and it is heading your way. This monster is out of control with rage and can't be talked to or reasoned with. But why is it so angry?

1. It's hungry and hunting for food.
2. It's searching for its lost love.
3. It's despondent because it's so ugly.
4. It's angry at the entire world.

KEY TO MONSTER!

(T) he monster in your imagination is a manifestation of the archetype known as the Shadow, representing the darker side to every person's personality. The Shadow is present in each of us, and the monster's anger is actually directed at a source of stress in our own life.

1. It's hungry and hunting for food.

The hungry monster is reacting to your own fight against your appetite. Have you been wrestling with a diet recently? It's hard to keep a clear head when you've got an empty stomach. Remember, everything in moderation, and that includes moderation itself. Better to have an occasional snack than to let the pressure build until you end up eating Tokyo.

2. It's searching for its lost love.

If you thought the monster was madly looking for its love, maybe you too have been going through some difficulties on the romantic front. Just keep reminding yourself, a love life without worries is no love life at all. Even Count Dracula had his off nights.

3. It's despondent because it's so ugly.

Those who thought the monster was consumed with rage at its own ugliness are dissatisfied with their own appearance in some way. Faults can become magnified in the mind's eye, and that negative self-image influences the way the rest of the world views us as well. The first step toward being loved is learning to love what you see when you look in the mirror.

4. It is angry at the entire world.

People who chose this answer have a pessimistic outlook. Not only is the glass half-empty, but the water is warm and tastes bad. It's good to be able to find mistakes that need correcting, but you'll never change the world just by complaining. Let's see if we can't find a way to put some of that energy to a more positive use.

THE LABYRINTH

Let's return once again to the amusement park to continue our explorations into the attractions of the unconscious mind. You're already familiar with some of the rides, the dizzying excitement of the roller coaster and the good-natured thrills of the merry-go-round. The house of horrors still lies waiting, but that's best left for couples to explore. How about a walk through the labyrinth instead?

You found your way through the giant maze and are standing at the exit. Which of these statements best describes how you feel?

1. "That was too easy. I was done in no time. What a piece of cake!"
2. "Well, it took a while to get through, but looking back, I guess it was really no big deal."
3. "Boy, was I lost! For a while there I thought I was never going to get out."
4. "I hooked up with a group of people inside and they showed me the way out. Otherwise I might still be in there."

KEY TO THE LABYRINTH

$\left(\text{T}\right)$he winding and circuitous paths of a maze represent the path you find for yourself in life, with all its false turns, backtracking, and dead ends. And adolescence is the time in life when it's easiest to feel lost and confused. Your experience in the labyrinth corresponds to the way you remember spending the years leading up to adulthood.

1. "That was too easy. I was done in no time. What a piece of cake!"

Although many people look back on their teenage years as a time of stress and confusion, for you it was nothing but fun. You weren't consumed with soul-searching or traumatized by peer pressure—actually the whole experience was like one big party. Of course, that may mean your true test in life still lies ahead. . . .

2. "Well, it took a while to get through, but looking back, I guess it was really no big deal."

Your school days were not easy for you, and it's more than likely you spent many a night worried over the same problems we all did—love, friendship, and the future. But that experience has helped to forge you into the person you are, and the lessons you learned will sustain you through any difficult times to come.

3. "Boy, was I lost! For a while there I thought I was never going to get out."

Although nearly everyone has a rough year or two growing up, you took worrying about life to the extremes, dwelling on problems that existed only in your head and torturing yourself with second guesses and self-doubt. That may have added a certain amount of seriousness and depth to your character, but now it's time for you to loosen up and enjoy life. You've earned it.

4. "I hooked up with a group of people inside and they showed me the way out. Otherwise I might still be in there."

The reason for the satisfaction you feel in life today lies with the friends you made and the relationships you formed during your youth. You had your worries like everyone else, but it seemed there was always someone for you to turn to when things got tough. Be grateful for the good luck you've had so far. Now it's your turn to return the favor and be there for others in need.

EMPTY INSIDE

S ome days everything just seems to go your way. Traffic seems to clear a path for you on the way to work; your boss takes the day off; you win the office pool. And you're all the happier because each new bit of luck comes as a pleasant surprise. Of course, there's another side to the unexpected as well. All it takes is a run in your stocking or a stain on your favorite tie to bring you right back down to grim reality. Good or bad, it's the little surprises that keep life interesting.

You go to a local bakery and buy a jelly doughnut. But when you get home and take a bite, you discover it's missing one essential ingredient—the jelly inside. How do you react to this bit of bad luck?

1. Take the defective doughnut back to the shop and get a new one.
2. Say to yourself, "These things happen," and eat the empty doughnut as is.
3. Eat something else.
4. Try filling the empty doughnut with something like maple syrup or jam to make it taste better.

KEY TO EMPTY INSIDE

 What do you call a jelly doughnut without any jelly in it?
A: A nasty surprise.

And while we're on the subject of the unexpected, you may be surprised to hear that the response you chose for this scenario shows the role you play among your friends.

1. Take the defective doughnut back to the shop and get a new one.

An orthodox thinker who isn't easily thrown off guard by odd occurrences, you can be relied on not to panic when the unexpected happens. But you aren't the type to take command and lead the way. Rather, you tend to support leader types with your clear judgment and coolheaded advice.

2. Say to yourself, "These things happen," and eat the empty doughnut as is.

You don't let surprises ruffle your feathers, accepting whatever hand the fates deal you. Your patience and flexibility make you incredibly easy to get along with, and it could be said you're the glue that holds your circle of friends together. Because you don't make a fuss over things, it sometimes seems that you fade into the background. But like air, you go unnoticed only until you're not around.

3. Eat something else.

Quick to make decisions and quick to act, you're a natural leader in any group. You come into your own when things get out of hand and the situation calls for one person to take charge and decide a course of action. You don't hem and haw over where to go for dinner or what movie to see—the word *indecision* is not in your vocabulary. That air of confidence and authority means that when you speak, the people around you listen.

4. Try filling the empty doughnut with something like maple syrup or jam to make it taste better.

Your talent for coming up with innovative solutions makes you the undisputed idea generator in your clique. Everyone has common sense, but you have a knack for uncommon sense that lets you see opportunities where others see only problems. Your creative instincts mean you run the risk of getting carried away with yourself and seeming eccentric from time to time, but people feel safe knowing that whatever may happen, you're sure to keep things interesting.

CIRCLE, TRIANGLE, SQUARE

Every shape and design may be reduced to the same basic building blocks: points and lines. For some, those words may dredge up painful buried memories of high school geometry class. But they can also take us back to a time when the world was simpler, to grade school art class when a house could be drawn using four squares and a triangle or a face created with a circle, two dots, and a wavy line. Our next quiz asks you to assume that innocent perspective and sense of creativity once more.

You'll need a pen and paper for this game. Using a single circle and any number of triangles and squares, draw a design on the paper.

KEY TO CIRCLE, TRIANGLE, SQUARE

(H) ow did your artwork turn out? Is it suitable for hanging on the refrigerator door? The real meaning of the design you drew can be found in your use of the three basic shapes. In this exercise the triangles represent work and study, the squares stand for society and its rules, and the lone circle is a symbol of yourself.

If you drew a very large circle, you possess an equally great sense of self. That can be a good thing when it leads to positive self-regard, but for some people it signifies a distorted notion of their place in the world—in other words, at its center. If you drew a very small circle, you see yourself as insignificant or dwarfed by the world around you. Don't let yourself be overwhelmed by all those triangles and squares; they're made of the same points and lines as you are!

The number and size of triangles you used represents your work or school responsibilities. Large triangles denote your sense of the importance of your work and the fulfillment you find in it, while a large number of triangles means you're working on several projects at once. Be careful if you have too many triangles; it may mean you need to cut down on your workload before it wears you out.

The squares in your design stand for how you feel about society and other people. If you used very large squares, it indicates you're under pressure to conform or fit in. If you put many squares in your design, it shows that you tend to feel lost in the crowd or burdened by too many rules.

If the shapes in your design connect, overlap, and share borders, it means you're enjoying a degree of integration and harmony between those aspects of your life. If all the shapes occupy separate spaces, it's likely you'll see signs of isolation and lack of connection in your life as well.

DOCTOR YOU

There's no escaping from desire. From the time we're children, we worry and want—I wish I were bigger, I want a new bike, I hope I don't fail the spelling test. The desire for a better life is in us all. And while it often leads to frustration and a sense of failure, that same desire is the driving force behind the successes we do achieve. Of course, no one succeeds in life alone. Everyone benefits at some point from a bit of wise advice, a kind word, or even a harsh critique. Think of all the times you yourself have been carried through a crisis supported by the words of others. If the time came for you to be the one giving support, what kind of job do you think you would do?

1. You are a psychotherapist with a private counseling service. In what kind of room do you hold your therapy sessions? Describe the room in detail.

2. Your first patient for the day has arrived. What problem does he or she want to talk over with you, and what kind of counsel do you give?

3. You sit across from the patient and give your professional advice. What kind of reaction do you get from the patient?

4. Office hours are done for the day, and you're at your desk doing paperwork when someone bursts in. Who is this person coming to you after hours? (Use the name of a person you know when answering.)

KEY TO DOCTOR YOU

$\left(H\right)$ ow did you do with your caseload for the day? The patient in this setting expresses the part of yourself that longs for support and guidance. Your answers give a picture of the things you feel are missing from your life.

1. The type of office you described indicates something you feel is missing from your life. Did you envision a quiet room for privacy and deep reflection? A bright environment where it's easy to get things out into the open? Was it a comfortable, nurturing space where you could feel safe? Or simply a large room where you could stretch your legs and relax? Where is your mind telling you you need to be?

2. The patient's complaint is actually a source of worry in your own mind. Was it a problem in the workplace? A dead-end romance? Perhaps a quest for personal growth?

The counseling you gave the patient is an answer to the problem facing you, from the clear-thinking, objective side of your mind. The question is, will you be able to take your own best advice?

3. The patient's reaction as you counseled shows whether you can accept good advice when it's offered to you. Was your patient hanging on every word you spoke or arguing with you stubbornly and refusing to take their own best interests to heart? Or did you

get the feeling that they were agreeing with what you were saying but would forget it all as soon as they stepped out the door?

4. The person who barged into your office after hours is the person in your life who causes you the most worry or stress. But that doesn't necessarily make that person a nuisance or someone to be avoided. Compassion for others is a mark of wisdom.

READY TO RUMBLE

Toe to toe in the ring, mountains of muscle and bone square off for the fight of the century. The wrestlers glower with menace and pace like caged beasts. The crowd roars with anticipation as its most aggressive fantasies are about to be played out.

No other sporting event has the elemental appeal of professional wrestling. We may laugh about it or shake our heads, but its popularity endures. If you had the chance to jump over that third rope, just for one night, what type of wrestler would you be? (Choose one of the following.)

1. A giant bruiser who bashes opponents into submission through sheer strength.

2. A technical wizard who invents elaborate clinches, drop kicks, and slams for each new opponent you face.

3. A villain type who resorts to illegal holds and banned objects every time the ref's back is turned.

4. An expressionless masked wrestler who never shows emotion or pain.

KEY TO READY TO RUMBLE

$\left(\text{S}\right)$ ports are a socially acceptable expression of natural human aggression, but on a deeper level they also represent a sublimation of the sex drive. And pro wrestling, with its wild abandon, its glorification of the body, its raw humanity, and its naked aggression has closer links to sex than any other sport. The type of wrestler you said you'd become shows the type of partner you are in bed.

1. A giant bruiser who bashes opponents to submission through sheer strength.

You insist on having things your way. Like the fighter who reduces his foe to a quivering mass, you take control of your partners and bend them to do your bidding without a second thought. It may sound brutal and animalistic, but then we aren't talking about a game of tiddlywinks, are we?

2. A technical wizard who invents elaborate clinches, drop kicks, and slams for each new opponent you face.

You enjoy trying out new tricks and techniques with each new partner. Part of the excitement in the game of love is generated by the freedom it gives you to express your creativity. You love to home in on your partner's most sensitive spot, then go in for the kill.

3. A villain type who resorts to illegal holds and banned items every time the ref's back is turned.

You can't be satisfied in making love by the book. You're always looking for new sensations, and you're not afraid to break a few rules (or introduce some forbidden objects) to get what you want. Now, just put down that folding chair before somebody gets hurt.

4. An expressionless masked wrestler who never shows emotion or pain.

You don't like to reveal your true self, even in the most intimate encounters. There's an aura of mystery to your lovemaking style, an almost eerie sense of calm. This tactic can drive some partners wild with curiosity or leave them feeling cold. But there will always come the day when your mask is finally torn away. Are you prepared to confront the face concealed beneath it?

JUDGING BY ITS COVER

Think of what it would be like to be the best-selling pop star in the world, the darling of the media and idol to millions. It's not such an uncommon fantasy to entertain as you sing along to the car radio or belt out hit after hit in the shower. You get a thrilling sense of satisfaction from being able to move people through the power of song.

You are a new recording artist, and you've just finished cutting your debut CD. Now all that remains is for you to decide on a cover design for the CD case. What type of jacket design would you pick?

1. A soothing scene using imagery or photos taken from some exotic location.

2. A fun, cartoonish design or other playful image.

3. An abstract pattern without any obvious meaning, but one that makes people think.

4. A picture of yourself.

KEY TO JUDGING BY ITS COVER

(T)he idea of releasing your own CD ties into the psychological need for self-expression. The design you'd like to see on your CD corresponds to those aspects of your personality that you want others to take notice of. Your choice can be interpreted as what you see as your own best attribute. Now let's see how the rest of the world views you. . . .

1. A scene relying on imagery or photos taken from some exotic location.

You see yourself as a caring and gentle person who always has a smile or kind word for others. As a matter of fact, it's hard to imagine how someone could be more sensitive than you. But to others, it sometimes seems as though you've got a wall around you that doesn't let anything get through to you, and all that sensitivity starts to look a little insincere. If you never let your guard down and show how you really feel, people will always be wondering what you're really thinking.

2. A fun, cartoonish design or other playful image.

You're sociable, talkative, and fun to be around. And you know it. But others see the flip side of that coin as well—unrealiable, flighty, and tending to get carried away by the moment. Being able to make people laugh is great, but it takes on a different meaning if they're laughing at you, not with you.

3. An abstract pattern without any obvious meaning, but one that makes people think.

You take pains to express your natural creativity and talent to the world. That talent may be there, but you need to remember that other people have their talents, too. The real way for you to shine is to accept and work together with others. Until you do, you risk being seen as strange. Your originality is important, but don't let it make you into just another crackpot eccentric.

4. A picture of yourself.

You take the straightforward approach, saying, "This is me, take me as I am," and you see that simple honesty as your strongest feature. But what you intend as honesty can come across as stubbornness—"This is me, I'm never going to change." Nobody's so great that they can't get better. If you want to keep the same image forever, at least make sure they get your good side.

BUSTED!

They say that police develop a sixth sense about the criminal mind. And each of us has a little bit of that criminal mind inside, which is why the police can never afford to be off duty. Murder, robbery, fraud—they're even more common than the newspapers make it seem. Not a minute goes by without a crime being committed or planned. If you were a cop, how do you think you'd handle the pressures of the beat?

You're in hot pursuit of a suspect fleeing a crime scene. After a long chase, you finally manage to run him down and make the arrest. You're standing over him with your pistol in his face. Busted! What does the suspect say to you as he stares down the barrel of your gun?

KEY TO BUSTED!

W hat did the cornered crook have to say for himself? Although you were imagining yourself as the police officer, your own hidden tendencies came out in the criminal's words. In the game of cops and robbers, it's the robbers who have to come up with excuses as the cops haul them off to jail. The way you imagined him responding gives an idea of how you reacted when your parents caught you doing something bad. And if you're like most people, it's how you continue to behave today.

"Okay, I give up. You got me. I'll talk." It's good for the conscience, and they might go easier on you come sentencing.

"You think you got me? I don't see any evidence. I want to talk to my lawyer." You may be able to slip through the cracks once or twice, but your wicked ways will catch up with you if you don't reform. Justice never sleeps.

DRIVING MACHINE

Remember practicing for your driver's license and all the little things you had to learn? U-turns, parallel parking, hand signals, and car lengths. . . . Sure, they're all important, but that isn't what driving is really all about. Driving is about the way you felt after passing those tests and taking to the road all by yourself for the very first time. It's about being able to go where you want, when you want. It's about power, freedom, and speed. And the car you drive is an expression of the way you view the whole driving experience. It tells the world something about who you are and what you want out of life.

Take a moment to picture your dream car, without giving any thought to expense or other practical considerations. What kind of car do you envision yourself in?

1. A high-performance vehicle with all the options.
2. A marvel of design with a sleek and beautiful chassis.
3. A status-symbol ride with a price tag to match.
4. Anything will do as long as it runs.

KEY TO DRIVING MACHINE

P eople's taste in cars typically reflects their taste in members of the opposite sex. The features you want in your dream car reveal the things you respond to when looking for a partner.

1. A high-performance vehicle with all the options.

Ideally you want everything out of your car and your partner, but that also means you're willing to appreciate the good points in everyone. Your wide range of tastes means you might look a little inconsistent, equally attracted to beauty, kindness, sophistication, humor, or charm. But that makes it possible for you to evaluate potential partners on their own strengths, giving you a basis for comparison before making your final choice.

2. A marvel of design with a sleek and beautiful chassis.

There's little doubt that physical appearance is the key to winning your heart. It's not only finding someone whose looks appeal to you that's important. You also want someone you can show off to the world. The exaggerated emphasis you place on the exterior means it's easy for you to end up with a real lemon. Always check under the hood before you drive anything home.

3. A status-symbol ride with a price tag to match.

Social position and material success are crucial to you, and that carries over to your choice of partners as well. The right family, the right school, the right career: for you they all add up to make the right person. Ambition is not a bad thing in itself, but your mate might not appreciate being just another rung on the ladder to your success.

4. Anything will do as long as it runs.

You're happy with just about anyone who meets certain minimum standards, which makes you open, accepting, and forgiving. You don't expect others to fulfill your dreams and enjoy the same consideration in return. That could be a smooth road to contentment. But when you think about it, it might mean others aren't really expecting much from you, either.

JUST CAN'T WAIT

S tarting work at a new job is always stressful: the unfamiliar people and environment, the million new things to be learned, the feeling of wanting to do a good job, and of course the inevitable goofs. We learn by making mistakes, then trying not to repeat them.

A friend of yours has just taken a job waiting tables at a restaurant. One day you decide to visit and see how the new job is going, but when you step inside you see your friend has gotten into some kind of trouble with one of the customers. What did your friend do wrong? (Choose one item from the menu below.)

1. Didn't come to the table even after being called several times.
2. Made a mistake taking the order and brought the wrong food.
3. Spilled something on the customer's clothes.
4. Started to clear the table before the customer had finished eating.

KEY TO JUST CAN'T WAIT

Y our friend in the restaurant is a psychological stand-in for you. The mistake you saw your friend make is rooted in your own unconscious recognition of a personal weakness of your own, particularly in terms of responding to the needs of others. The mistakes you imagined your friend making are the very problems you find in your own love life.

1. Didn't come to the table even after being called several times.

You see yourself as lacking in the ability to concentrate and focus yourself on your partner. When out for the night, you might simply just wander away from your date when you see something that catches your fancy. Or maybe you're always getting caught with your eyes looking where they shouldn't be. That lack of focus might be interpreted as a lack of caring, so try to pay a little more attention. . . . Hello? Are you listening?

2. Made a mistake taking the order and brought the wrong food.

You come up short in the personal responsibility department. Maybe this manifests itself as always being late or in bringing along uninvited friends to what was planned as an evening for two. If romances are like a contract between two people, you've committed more than your share of breaches. If you want a happier love life, make a stronger policy of thinking about your partner's feelings before you do something.

3. Spilled something on the customer's clothes.

You're too nervous when it comes to dating. You want everything to be perfect and for everything to go smoothly, but it's difficult for others to relax when you make such a fuss over every last detail. You might make a good first impression by being so serious, but it's easy to see how people could quickly get tired of the high stress level.

4. Started to clear the table before the customer had finished eating.

You tend to jump the gun when it comes to love. That eagerness may seem charming at first, but after a while it just feels as though you're always chomping at the bit. Slow down and let your partner have a chance to breathe, or you may find yourself with nothing but time on your hands.

ON SECOND THOUGHT . . .

I t's not easy to make up a story, it's a chore to make up the bed in the guestroom, and it takes patience and forgiveness to make up after a fight, but sometimes the hardest thing to make up is your mind. Get ready to be decisive, because in this next scenario we're going to ask you to do just that.

You're seated in a quiet diner. You flip open the menu and are pondering your selection when the waitress arrives and asks if you're ready to order. Without thinking, you order a sandwich and a cup of coffee. But after she leaves, it comes to you—you're in the mood for hot chocolate, not coffee! What do you do next?

1. Keep looking through the menu and thinking about how good some hot cocoa would taste.
2. Look around to see if the waitress is going to come back.
3. Get up and find the waitress so you can change your order.
4. Give up and just wait for the coffee.

KEY TO ON SECOND THOUGHT . . .

(G) ranted, making a mistake when you order is not the end of the world. You'll probably have forgotten the whole thing a half hour from now. But the way you handled your mistake with the cocoa tells us something deeper about your personality. Your course of action (or inaction) shows how you would react to a relationship ending. Specifically it shows how long you carry a torch for a love gone wrong.

1. Keep looking through the menu and thinking about how good some hot cocoa would taste.

You're the type that doesn't know when to call it quits. You keep dwelling on the good times and fantasizing that someday things will get back to the way they were. Odds are they won't. The fat lady sang, and the curtain is already down. It's time to wake up and smell the coffee.

2. Look around to see if the waitress is going to come back.

You're not all that thrilled about the breakup, but you definitely don't want to make a scene. In a nutshell, you worry too much about what other people think. You're more concerned that people might be whispering about your getting dumped than you are about the actual breakup. Come to think of it, that pride of yours might have been the reason you got dumped in the first place.

3. Get up and find the waitress so you can change your order.

You're not the sort who gets mired down in romantic mourning and a sense of loss after a romance ends—mainly because it's completely inconceivable that that kind of thing could have happened to you. Your reaction is more a state of shock than mourning, and you'll do anything to try to make the memory go away. Maybe you should take up a hobby to take your mind off things.

4. Give up and just wait for the coffee.

Is that "Que Sera, Sera" playing on the jukebox? It might as well be, because that's your theme song. It generally takes you one night's sleep to get over a breakup. A power nap would probably do in a pinch. The question is whether that makes you thick-skinned, insensitive, or the most unshakable optimist in the world.

THE DOCTOR WILL SEE YOU NOW

A hospital means different things to different people. Those coming in to have some undiagnosed malady examined for the first time may look on the place with a sense of anxiety and dread. But for those walking out the door after recovering from a long illness or delivering a beautiful, healthy baby, the hospital takes on associations of happiness and relief. The hospital is a world in itself, where life and death, sadness and joy, cross paths and intermingle on a daily basis. And for the people within, every day is another chance to heal not just the body, but the mind as well.

Perhaps you have been to the hospital before, or perhaps this is your first visit. Either way prepare yourself, because the doctor will see you now.

1. You're in the lobby of a medical clinic, waiting for your name to be called. A small boy is racing around the waiting area unattended, and you warn him to be careful and slow down. How does he react?

2. The door to the examination room is open just a crack, and you catch a glimpse of a gray and unhealthy-looking person being examined by the doctor. The patient is a person you know. Who is it?

3. The doctor's aide comes out and calls your name. Strangely, the aide bears a very strong resemblance to someone you know. Whom does the aide look like?

4. After your examination, the doctor calls you into his office, but when you enter he remains seated with his back turned to you, muttering to himself as he goes over your chart. He shows no signs of explaining things to you. What do you do?

KEY TO THE DOCTOR WILL SEE YOU NOW

T he hospital is a place of sickness and healing. By visualizing yourself in this scenario, you tapped into those parts of your own psychology that feel weak or in need of care.

1. The boy's reaction shows how you react when others criticize you or notice your faults. Did he act as though he couldn't hear you, stop in his tracks and apologize, or stick out his tongue like a spoiled brat? Now you understand how other people feel.

2. The person you imagined as the patient on the exam table is someone you feel you could never rely on in a crisis. After all, how much help could they be if they look that much sicker than you?

3. The doctor's aide represents someone with the power to decide your fate. The person you thought the aide resembled is someone you have always looked up to, out of either fear or respect. No matter how strong you may someday become, that person will always be above you in your mind. It might have to do with the person's power to say, "Now drop your pants, bend over, and cough."

4. The way you responded to the doctor's behavior shows how you handle being bullied or teased. Some prefer to wait things out, others demand an explanation, and some just get up and walk out the door. What did you do?

SPREADING YOUR WINGS

I n times of stress and frustration, it's normal and natural for people to want to shed their troubles and leave the world behind. Think about it. When you love someone who doesn't love you back, or things just aren't going your way at work, sometimes the easiest solution is to get as far away as possible until the feeling fades. Getting away gives you the chance to free your mind and do the things you want to do. But as much as we'd like to drop everything and walk out the door, it's easier to dream about than to do. Maybe that's what makes us turn to the heavens for relief—we all just want a chance to fly and be free.

1. You have decided to try skydiving and are getting ready to make your first jump. You watch other skydivers free-falling through the air as you stand on the ground waiting your turn. What is going through your mind?

2. Your turn arrives, and you ready yourself as the plane climbs to ten thousand feet. Without looking back, you stand at the open doorway and step out into space. What do you scream on your way down?

3. You've landed safely and are hauling in your chute when you see an instructor approaching and calling out to you. What is the instructor saying?

KEY TO SPREADING YOUR WINGS

(D)id you enjoy your little walk in the clouds? The pure adrenaline rush of a skydiving adventure relates to physical thrills of a different sort—the thrill of sex. The things you said about your parachuting experience actually describe your approach to lovemaking.

1. The way you felt as you waited your turn provides a measure of your own level of sexual desire.

"This is gonna be fun. I can't wait!" Sometimes it just feels right.

"I don't know if I can go through with this." If you're not sure you're ready, maybe you can just have a deep conversation and cuddle by the fire.

2. The words you shouted on the way down are what you would say at the peak of excitement.

"Wow, would you look at this view!" You may not mind the intrusion on your privacy, but you'd better ask your partner first.

"Maybe this wasn't such a good idea after all." There is such a thing as a point of no return.

"I want my mommy!" Um, let's just say you have some deep Kokological issues to work out and leave it at that.

3. The words the instructor said to you are what you imagine your partner saying after sex.

"Not bad for a beginner. Don't worry, you'll get better with practice!"

"Oh, I'm really sorry, I left the lens cap on the camera. Do you want to go again?"

"Well, I guess that about does it. Now, will that be cash, check, or charge?"

ALL THE WORLD'S A STAGE

L ife is often compared to a drama—it's an easy comparison to make. The coming and going of the characters, the suspense as each day's plot unfolds, the lines we hear spoken, and the acts performed: you could say we live each day on stage. There are even genres to the stories—office comedies and after-school specials, sometimes even a mystery or romance. And the star of each daily episode is . . . you! That's what makes life's drama so fascinating and endlessly varied—every cast member in every scene, every extra on the street, is the star of his or her own story in a plot that gets more complex every day. Even the simplest exchange between two people can have infinite implications as the drama plays out. Maybe that's why, despite the same old characters and story lines, we can never seem to get enough. In this next scenario the curtain is up, the crowd is waiting, and the spotlight is on you.

1. You are a member of a theater group. What type of play do you most want to act in? In the play, what do you picture as your big scene? Explain in detail.

2. You audition for the part and are chosen from among all your fellow performers for the starring role. What words does your main rival have for you on being chosen?

3. At the last dress rehearsal before opening night, you see the director sitting with his arms crossed in front of him. He looks dissatisfied with your performance. What is it he doesn't like?

4. The performance goes off without a hitch, and the play was a huge success. The crowd has gone home happy after the encore, and the theater is quiet. What do you say to the empty hall as you stand there looking out from the darkened stage?

KEY TO ALL THE WORLD'S A STAGE

(T) he theater represents a world of imagination you create for yourself. Your answers to this game reveal what lies waiting in your own future.

1. The type of drama you wanted to perform corresponds to your future. Did you foresee a melodrama, a tragedy, or a slapstick pie fight? And your big scene reveals what you predict will be the turning point in your life. If it was a love scene, there may be a romantic lead waiting to change your life. Was it a scene of parting with friends, of meeting new people, or of a heated battle? These all could be the cues for you to take center stage and make your command performance.

2. The image you have of your rival reflects how your future self might react to the person you are today. The rival's words give an idea of how you think you will feel while looking back on your life when you're older. Was your response something encouraging like "Nice going! Keep up the good work!" Or was there a sense of caution: "Don't get a big head. One good show doesn't make you a star. You've still got a long way to go till you make it to the big time."

3. The director watches every aspect of the performance with a cold and objective eye. His dissatisfaction was caused by a weak-

ness you unconsciously recognize in yourself. The flaw in your performance represents the area in which you're most likely to make mistakes in the future.

If he said your character was getting lost in all the scenery, you may need to work harder at standing up for yourself in life. Who's the star of this show, anyway?

On the other hand, if he told you that you were hogging the stage, you might want to try toning things down a notch. Nobody likes a ham.

If he told you your timing was off, be careful not to miss opportunities that come knocking in your life. There are no chances to redo a scene in the real world.

And if he said you just weren't exciting to watch, you should try to liven yourself up a little. If even you can't sit through your performance, think how the rest of the world feels.

4. Your words to the empty theater are the words you picture yourself saying at the end of your life. Recognize any of these famous last words?

"Thank God that's over! I need a drink!" An understandable sentiment, but there aren't any bars where you're headed.

"I couldn't have done it without the little people." It's good to remember the people who helped us on the way.

"That wasn't so bad." Maybe that's the best parting line that any of us can hope to be able to say.

"Look out, world, here I come." Just where is it exactly that you think you're going?